Welcome to New York

D1540280

SEP 12 2018

917.471
Micheli
2018

One World Trade Center
© DelensMode/Moment RM/Getty Images

Getting to New York

FROM JOHN F. KENNEDY (JFK)

♿ *www.panynj.gov/airports/jfk.html*
24 km/15mi southwest of Manhattan.

Shuttle – go to Ground Transportation. $20-25 per person and 1hr-1hr30min.

Taxi – 40-90min depending on traffic. Set price for Manhattan $52, 80 cent surcharge, $4.50 rush hour surcharge, plus tip ($1-2).

Car services – Lyft, Juno, Via, and Uber all pick up at JFK. Prices vary depending on whether you share a car or take a private ride. Expect to pay minimum $30 to Manhattan.

NY Airport Service – Links to (every 20-30min), Penn Station, Port Authority and Grand Central. At Grand Central, there are shuttles for guests staying in hotels located between 23rd and 63rd Sts. $18. 1hr-1hr30min. www.nycairporter.com

Subway – Take the **AirTrain** to the subway. Depending on your destination, take the **A**, **J**, or **E** lines. Expect 60min on subway. Faster is taking the **LIRR** (regional train) to either **Penn Station** (if your destination is in Manhattan) or **Atlantic Terminal** (if in Brooklyn). Air Train : $5 plus $2.75 for the subway; LIRR: $7.75.

Queensboro Bridge
© B. Rieger/hemis.fr

FROM LAGUARDIA (LGA)

♿ *laguardiaairport.com*
13 km/8mi east of the city centre.
Shuttle - Follow signs for Ground Transportation. Expect $20 per person and 30-45min.
Taxi – Expect $35-55 for Manhattan, plus tip and around 30min.
Car services and NY Airport Service– Same as JFK

FROM NEWARK (EWR)

♿ *www.panynj.gov/airports/newark-liberty.html*
26 km/16mi southeast of Manhattan, in New Jersey.

Taxi – Expect $40-70, plus tip and surcharge of $5 at rush hour, and 45min-1hr.
Train – The **AirTrain** links to the trains connecting Newark to New York (Penn Station). Combined AirTrain + New Jersey Transit ticket: $13.
Car services – Same as JFK.

Unmissable

Our picks for must-see sites

Greenwich Village★★
Map A-B6 - ♿ p. 40

Museum of Modern Art★★★
Map C4 - ♿ p. 58

Central Park★★★
Map D3, C-D4, E2 -
♿ p. 67

**Metropolitan Museum
of Art★★★**
Map D3 - ♿ p. 74

**One World
Observatory★★★**
Map A8 - ♿ p. 18

4

Empire State Building★★★
Map C5 - 🖑 p. 54

Brooklyn Bridge★★★
Map B8 - 🖑 p. 26

Soho★★
Map B7 - 🖑 p. 32

Times Square★★
Map C5 - 🖑 p. 53

Statue of Liberty★★★
Map A8 - 🖑 p. 22

5

Our top picks

💜 **Sip a cocktail in a bar with a view**. Grab a sundowner at one of New York's many rooftop terraces and marvel at the panoramic view over the city 👤 *p. 114, 115, 116 & 117*.

💜 **Take a break in a pocket park**. Tucked away in one of the city's many pint-sized pocket parks , secluded from the hubbub, you'll hear only birdsong and the sound of running water. An ideal quiet spot for a break. 👤 *p. 66*.

💜 **Follow the stars of the silver screen**. Take the family on a trip to the Museum of the Moving Image in Astoria, Queens. 👤 *p. 100*.

💜 **Go to a gospel service in Harlem** on a Sunday morning. Expect impassioned sermons and rousing song. Finish the morning back on earth with a brunch in the neighborhood. 👤 *p. 126 & 142*.

💜 **Go to an outdoor market in Brooklyn.** Grab a veggie burger and fresh fruit juice and have lunch on the grass while admiring the view of Manhattan. Spend the morning soaking in the hipster Brooklyn vibe and perusing the stalls of vintage clothing, re-purposed furniture and hand-made jewelry. 👤 *p. 123*.

💜 **Pay homage to Frank Lloyd Wright** and the magnificent spiral ramp that has made the Guggenheim Museum recognized the world over. 👤 *p. 80*.

💜 **Recharge in the quiet medieval gardens of the Cloisters**, with a view out over the Hudson River. Your backdrop is the stones of cloisters shipped from Europe and reconstructed stone by stone. 👤 *p. 94*.

💜 **Breathe in the fresh air in Riverside Park.** Abundant nature and great views over the Hudson are on offer. Cycle along the water or go for

6

© JeffreyFina/iStockphoto.com

The Cloisters

© L. Deccudin/Michelin

7

Rooftop of Boom Boom Room

your weekly (annual?) run; children will love the playgrounds and skate parks. Nearby are the Museum of Natural History ♿ *p. 86* and Children's Museum of Manhattan.

💙 **Watch the sun set from Tudor City Place at the eastern end of 42ⁿᵈ St.** This is also one of the best spots to contemplate the Chrysler Building. ♿ *p. 64.*

💙 **Feel tiny under the 55-ft Barosaurus skeleton at the American Museum of Natural History.** The rich collection here will delight children, taking them on a journey back in time, and is one of the largest of its kind in the world. ♿ *p. 86.*

💙 **Bulgogi, barbecue, and karaoke.** Explore Koreatown for delicious eats like smoky Korean barbecue followed by karaoke, or pick up ingredients at one of the Korean supermarkets ♿ *p. 56.*

💙 **Visit the Whitney Museum** of American Art, designed by Renzo Piano. The space thrills with its bright modular galleries and terraces on each level, with views over the High Line. ♿ *p. 46.*

New York in 3 days

Beyond Manhattan

Take a jaunt to Queens and take in the contemporary art at PSI★ (p. 99), or head to the family-friendly Museum of the Moving Image★★ (p. 100). Fill up at Ornella (p. 111) before hopping over to Brooklyn. Start with a walk in Brooklyn Heights★★ (p. 95), with breathtaking views of Manhattan, then spend the evening discovering the hot spots of Williamsburg★ (p. 110, 117 & 126). Be sure to grab a cocktail at Ides Bar (p. 117), the rooftop bar of the chic and ultra-hip Wythe Hotel.

8

DAY 1

▶ Morning
Start your day by taking in the topography of New York from the top of the **Empire State Building**★★★ (p. 54) or the **Top of the Rock**★★★ (p. 58).

▶ Midday
Stop at Café Serai (p. 108) in the **Rubin Museum**★★ (p. 46); or picnic with goods from **Chelsea Market** (p. 108). You can get your food to go and stroll the **High Line**★★ (p. 47).

▶ Afternoon
Tour the galleries ★★ (p. 45) of Chelsea, before exploring **Greenwich Village**★★ (p. 40) and the **Meatpacking District**★ (p. 45).

▶ Evening
Stay in Meatpacking for a drink with a view on the terrace of **The Top of The Standard** (p. 115) or get dinner in the **Lower East Side**★ (p. 106), another trendy neighborhood.

DAY 2

▶ Morning
Set off early to get up close to the **Statue of Liberty**★★★ (p. 22). When you arrive back in Manhattan, walk into the **Financial District**★★ (p. 20).

▶ Afternoon
Visit the site of the **World Trade Center**★★★ (p. 14). Check out **South Seaport Street Historic District**★★ (p. 26), New York's first port, before walking across the **Brooklyn Bridge** (p. 26) where the views over Manhattan are unforgettable.

▶ Evening
Spend an evening in **Greenwich Village**★★ (p. 42, 106 and 125), a lively neighborhood full of great spots to wine and dine.

Where are the clubs?

Club kids can head to Meatpacking and Chelsea, where you'll find veteran nightclubs. Or, try the Berlin-style trappings of Output (p. 126) in Williamsburg, one of the best dance clubs on the East Coast.

© L. Cecoudin/Miche in

Museum of the Moving Image, Queens

DAY 3

▶ *Morning*

Arty morning at the **Met**★★★ *(p. 74)*.

▶ *Midday*

Have a picnic under the trees of **Central Park**★★★ *(p. 67 & 109)*, or opt for the Roof Garden Café at the Met.

▶ *Afternoon*

Continue your cultured day at the **MoMA**★★★ *(p. 58)*. If you still have energy left and cash in your pocket, do a spot of shopping between Madison and **5th Avenue**★★★ *(p. 54)*.

▶ *Evening*

Get a little bit of rest before your night out on **Broadway**★ *(p. 51)*. Catch a 7pm show and then get lost among

A fourth day?

*Brush up on your painting knowledge at the **Frick Collection**★★★ (p. 71), then get lunch at **Isabella's** (p. 109). In the afternoon, visit the **Museum of Natural History**★★★ (p. 86). Alternatively, swap a museum for a wander in **Riverside Park**★★ (p. 90) or a shopping session in **Soho**★★ (p. 32 and 119). Let your evening meal transport you with dinner in **Koreatown** (p. 56) or **Chinatown**★★ (p. 28 and p. 104).*

the neon signs of **Times Square**★★ *(p. 53)*. For a quick and inexpensive dinner, indulge in a burger at Shake Shack *(p. 108)*.

Disovering New York

High Line Park
© A. Armellin/Sime/Photononstop

New York today

The writer E. B. White wasn't wrong when he said, "There are roughly three New Yorks. There is, first, the New York of the man or woman who was born here, who takes the city for granted and accepts its size and its turbulence as natural and inevitable. Second, there is the New York of the commuter — the city that is devoured by locusts each day and spat out each night. Third, there is the New York of the person who was born somewhere else and came to New York in quest of something. Commuters give the city its tidal restlessness; natives give it solidity and continuity; but the settlers give it passion."

New York is entirely different from the rest of America. Either way, to come to New York is to experience an **unforgettable shock to the system:** the city leaves no one indifferent. For many, getting lost amid the colorful avenues and boulevards that literature, cinema and music have made so familiar is enough to fall in love with the place immediately, and for life. There is much to charm: crossing the man-made canyons created between the gleaming cliffs of the skyscrapers; soaking in the cosmopolitan ambiance in the old neighborhoods of Chinatown and Harlem; jogging in Central Park; or seeing the skyline of Manhattan suddenly appear across the East River as you cross Brooklyn Bridge The "vertical city", as French writer Céline called it, is full of paradoxes. The megalopolis overspills with vitality despite the trauma of 9/11. The city is at once coarse and sophisticated, of-the-people and elitist, typically American and still different from any other American city. As for New Yorkers themselves, they consider their city to be beyond doubt the most beautiful, most important and most "everything" city in the world.

It's hard to disagree. The frenetic rhythm of the city will draw you in immediately, making you feel that something important is happening– that you are at the center of the world. It's a **whirlwind** of light, sound and movement. Amid surging cars, howling sirens, incessant construction, whirring air conditioning units and the fractured hubbub of the city, the noise level never really goes down, not even at night (despite the Silent Night initiative brought in by former mayor Michael Bloomberg, which didn't succeed in changing much).

The first visual impression of the city is one of irrepressible vitality, almost aggression. The sharp-lined skyscrapers, one shamelessly out-climbing the next, don't feign any attempt at harmony. The competition and one-upmanship of the cityscape creates a jagged **kaleidoscope** of mismatched shapes with only one aim: do better; build higher, build more expensive. Observers have often characterized this aesthetic as masculine, even phallic: think vertical pillars of concrete and glass that enveloped passers-by in their vast shadow. You can always tell the tourists because they're the only ones looking up as they walk: New Yorkers have better things to do.

To discover New York is to go on an **adventure**, immersing yourself in this hyperactive maelstrom of contrasts. The unchanging familiarities of the Old World are forgotten here: the city advances relentlessly, and will continue to do so, whatever comes. If you think you know fast traffic, prepare to think again when you arrive in New York. **Taxi drivers** will not contradict even the most exaggerated Hollywood depictions of their profession; the buses seem to be engaged in a car chase. The pace of the city is undeniable: New Yorkers never stop. The sometimes overwhelming noise in the middle of the night of sirens, construction, and bar-goers will remind you that in this town, every minute counts.

New Yorkers, of course, walk fast. They know where they're going; they're busy; they have three times more things to do than the 24 hours of the day could possibly allow. Make sure you keep pace!

© Jcn Arnold/herris.fr

13

Times Square

On the sidewalk, pedestrians follow one another and walk on the right. This is the only place where everyone does the same thing. Discipline is essential: it's the only way the rush hour hoards can avoid hurting each other.

Now that you have the keys, the rest is up to you. Surviving in the **whirlwind** that is New York can feel like making your way through a jungle. But you will soon start to feel at ease here. After a few short hours, you'll find yourself magically carried along by the city's irrepressible vitality.

Lower Manhattan★★

The city as we know it began right here. The legendary skyline contrasts with old cobbled streets, all punctuated with symbolic sites: the World Trade Center, with its poignant memories; the Brooklyn Bridge; Wall Street and the New York Stock Exchange, the global nucleus of finance and, in the distance, the familiar silhouette of the Statue of Liberty.

Access: Subway: all stations between Chambers St. and South Ferry (lines 1 to 6, E, J, R, W, Z). Bus: M9, M15, M20, M22, M55, M103 all have stops in Lower Manhattan. The red Downtown Connection bus is **free** and runs throughout Lower Manhattan. *www.downtownny.com*
***Area map p. 16-17**. **Detachable map AB8**.*
▶**Tip:** for great photos of the skyscrapers, head to Brooklyn Bridge in the morning. At night, admire the illuminated skyline from Brooklyn Heights. Advance booking is advisable for visiting the Federal Reserve Bank or City Hall.

14

The first European colonists, the Dutch, settled on the southern tip of Manhattan and established a large farming village. The original layout of that village has been partially conserved, meaning you won't find the city's characteristic grid, but rather streets that run odd angles. The settlement quickly became a busy commercial port, first under **Dutch control** (&⃝ *p. 152*), and then English. However, the markets were unstable as a result of ongoing political unrest and violence. In 1792, 16 years after the Declaration of Independence was signed, financiers decided to establish New York's first stock market with the money made from property speculation. You'll still find vestiges of the early city at Fraunces Tavern, James Watson House and Trinity Church, and a few remaining cobbled streets. On the other end of the spectrum, the New World Trade Center is a powerful reminder of the tragedy of September 11th.

WORLD TRADE CENTER★★★

New York and the United States changed forever on **September 11, 2001**, when two planes, hijacked and rerouted by terrorists, crashed into the twin towers of the **World Trade Center**. One hour and forty minutes later, they collapsed on themselves; the world looked on horrified as the proudest symbols of American prosperity were swallowed up in a cloud of dust.
Two 110-story structures disappeared, taking with them 2973 victims.

Statue of Liberty and Lower Manhattan skyline

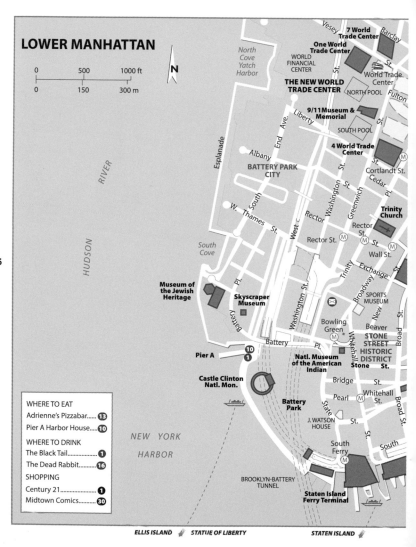

LOWER MANHATTAN

N

| 0 | 500 | 1000 ft |
| 0 | 150 | 300 m |

North Cove Yatch Harbor

Vesey St

7 World Trade Center

Barclay St.

One World Trade Center

WORLD FINANCIAL CENTER

THE NEW WORLD TRADE CENTER

World Trade Center

NORTH POOL

Fulton St.

Liberty St.

9/11 Museum & Memorial

SOUTH POOL

4 World Trade Center

Cortlandt St. (M)

Cedar Pl.

Albany St.

Esplanade

End Ave.

BATTERY PARK CITY

Washington St.

Greenwich St.

Trinity Church

HUDSON RIVER

South End Ave.

Rector St.

W. Thames St.

West St.

Rector St. (M)

Rector St. (M)

Wall St.

South Cove

Exchange

Trinity Pl.

Broadway

Museum of the Jewish Heritage

Skyscraper Museum

Washington St.

SPORTS MUSEUM

Bowling Green (M)

STONE STREET HISTORIC DISTRICT

Beaver St.

New St.

Broad St.

Battery Pl.

Battery

Pier A

10
1

Natl. Museum of the American Indian

Stone St.

Castle Clinton Natl. Mon.

Bridge St.

Whitehall St.

Pearl St.

Battery Park

J. WATSON HOUSE

State St.

Broad St.

NEW YORK HARBOR

South Ferry (M)

South St.

WHERE TO EAT
Adrienne's Pizzabar...... **13**
Pier A Harbor House.....**10**

WHERE TO DRINK
The Black Tail...............**1**
The Dead Rabbit...........**16**

SHOPPING
Century 21.....................**1**
Midtown Comics...........**30**

BROOKLYN-BATTERY TUNNEL

Staten Island Ferry Terminal

16

ELLIS ISLAND 🚢   STATUE OF LIBERTY   STATEN ISLAND 🚢

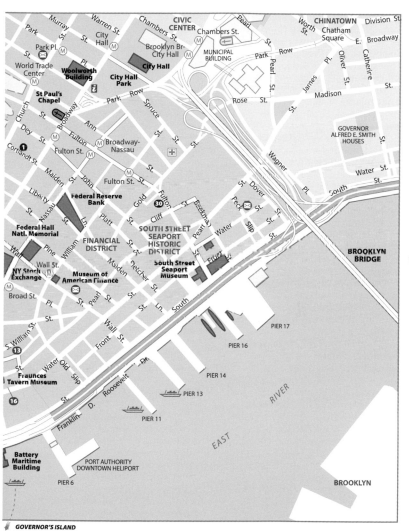

17

GOVERNOR'S ISLAND

Finished in 1973, after eleven years of construction works, the towers rose to 411m/1348ft (more or less double the height of all the surrounding towers) and accounted for 16% of the office space in Downtown. Around 50 000 people worked there.

The project – None of the proposed projects, even the one that was eventually taken up, proved to be entirely satisfactory. The initial plans of **Daniel Libeskind** were modified by the architect **David Childs**, so much so that the first stone, laid with great pomp in 2004, had to be replaced in 2006. There will be six new towers in the place of the seven buildings destroyed in the attacks, with building works slated to finish in 2020. The south-east of the site offers the best view of the ongoing construction and best vantage point to take in its enormous size. On the corner of **Church and Vesey Streets**, parts of each tower are preserved behind high railings with sober plaques referring to the tragedy. **One World Trade Center** (1 WTC), formerly Freedom Tower, stands at 541m/1776ft, a reference to the date of the Independence of the United States. Today it stands alongside 7 WTC (inaugurated in 2006) and 4 WTC (inaugurated in 2013) and will soon be neighbored by 3 WTC *(175 Greenwich St. – completion date unknown)*, 5 WTC *(130 Liberty St.)*, 2 WTC *(200 Greenwich St. – completion slated for 2022)*. 2 WTC will be the city's second largest skyscraper and will feature a diamond-shaped roof.

One World Observatory★★★ – *One World Trade Center - 285 Fulton St. - ✆ (844) 696 1776 - https:// oneworldobservatory.com - daily 9am-8pm (last tickets sold at 7.15pm) - $34 (over 65s $32, 6-12 years $28).* The observatory on the 102nd fl. is reached by the Sky Pod, one of the fastest elevators in the world: during the ascent (57 seconds) the evolution of the Manhattan skyline from 17C to present, is retraced on the walls of the elevator. From the top, the 360°-view over Manhattan, 380m/1247ft up, is breathtaking. On a clear day, the view stretches 80km/50mi in every direction. The view will help you get a feel for the geography of the city, with its long spits of land, hemmed in by water.

9/11 Museum & Memorial★★ – *entry via 1 Albany St. (corner of Greenwich St.) - ✆ 212 266 5211 - www.911memorial.org - museum: Sun-Thur. 9am-8pm last entry at 6pm), Fri-Sat 9am-9pm (last entry at 7pm); memorial : daily 7.30am-9pm hours subject to variation, check online before your visit - advance booking essential (online) - $ 24 ($18 over 65s, $ 15/7-17 years).* The underground museum takes you into the guts of the WTC. Here, thousands of artifacts related to the tragedy are exhibited, spanning objects such as a partially-burned ID card and a fire truck melted out of shape by the unimaginable heat. Photos and videos punctuate the visit and homage is paid to each of the 2973 victims killed in the attacks. Visitors can listen to various impossibly heartbreaking sound recordings, including the deeply affecting messages left by future victims, stuck in the burning towers or on the planes. The management of the museum, however, have also faced some criticism. There were accusations that the exhibits did not present the global geopolitical situation seriously enough; there was also controversy surrounding the decision to include a gift shop, which many found inappropriate. Most contentiously, there were mixed reactions following the decision to place the unidentified remains of victims on the site, in the bedrock 70ft (21m) below ground. The memorial, *Reflecting the Absence*, by architect **Michael Arad**, is made up of two 9m/30ft-deep pools down which run vast man-made waterfalls. They are surrounded by bronze panels engraved with the names of each of the victims. More than 400 oak trees are planted around the basins, giving the site a calm and serene atmosphere, conducive to quiet contemplation.

One tree distinguishes itself from the others: a pear tree, recovered from the debris after the attacks. Today, visitors gather round it to touch the bark of the "miracle tree", a symbol of hope and regeneration.

Station – The World Trade Center station was designed by Santiago Calatrava. Recognizable by its vast steel wings, it is meant to welcome more than 250 000 people a day, and features a huge shopping center, measuring 111m/364ft in length and 49m/160ft in height.

CITY HALL★

www.nyc.gov - guided tour 1hr - first-come, first-served tours Wed. 10am (register the day before between 10am and 11.30am at the welcome desk) and by reservation Thurs 10am

(℘ *212 788-2656; tours@cityhall.nyc. gov*). Recognizable by its high clock tower, City Hall is one of New York's most elegant buildings. Its Georgian interior (1812) is housed behind a fine marble facade, inspired by the French Renaissance. The architects, not knowing the city would spread north, made the back of the building in brown sandstone; it was only in 1956 that it was covered in Alabama limestone.

CITY HALL PARK★

It was here in what was a field of apple trees that the Declaration of Independence was read in July 1776.

WOOLWORTH BUILDING★★

233 Broadway. Erected in 1913 by architect **Cass Gilbert** for **Frank Woolworth**, who owned a large chain of shops, this 241m/790ft edifice would remain until 1930 the world's tallest skyscraper, when the Chrysler Building was completed. With its stunning profusion of gargoyles and pinnacles and green clock-tower-adorned roof, it's considered one of the city's greatest architectural works. Its spectacular lobby mixes Gothic and Byzantine frescoes and mosaics.

SAINT PAUL'S CHAPEL

www.trinitywallstreet.org - 10am-6pm, services Sunday 8am and 9.15am. The oldest church in Manhattan (1766), constructed in the Georgian style in vogue in London at the time. Fire fighters and rescue workers came

Wall Street

© P. Adams/Danita Delimont Agency/age fotostock

here to rest and clean up following the attacks on the World Trade Center.

FINANCIAL DISTRICT★★

Wall Street – It takes its name from the wall that protected the Dutch settlement. Knocked down by the English in 1699, it was replaced by a road which would become the emblem of American capitalism. Lined by beautiful Georgian buildings, Wall Street emerged as an important financial center in the 19C; in 1920, it became the world's leading stock exchange, ahead of London. It has not been surpassed since, despite the crashes of 1929, 1987 and 2008. In the wake of these crises, many office buildings were left unoccupied and turned into housing.

New York Stock Exchange (NYSE) – This elegant 17-storey edifice (1903) houses the **New York Stock Exchange**. It is constructed in the style of a classical temple, with Corinthian columns and a pediment featuring allegorical sculpted figures representing commerce.

Stone Street Historic District★ – Between Wall Street and the East River, this was the first paved road in Manhattan. A protected site since 1996, it has conserved its old-world charm with its brick buildings crisscrossed with painted metal staircases and very contemporary happy hour bars.

Federal Hall National Memorial★ – *26 Wall St. - ℘ 212 825 6990 - www. nps.gov/feha - daily except weekends 9am-5pm - closed Thanksgiving and 25 Dec - free.* Located close to the NYSE, this edifice in the style of a temple is built on the site of New York's first City Hall, constructed in 1699 and then used as a law court. Redesigned after Independence, it became **Federal Hall**, the headquarters of the first United States Congress. It is here that George Washington was sworn in as president, a scene acted out by his statue here. The current building, which dates from 1842, housed US Customs and then the Treasury.

Museum of American Finance – *48 Wall St. - ℘ 212 908 4693 - www. moaf.org - daily except Sun and Mon 10am-4pm - $8 (under 6s free).* Since 2008, this museum has occupied the former headquarters of the **Bank**

of New York, founded in 1784 by Alexander Hamilton. The permanent collection brings together documents on the history of Wall Street, the crash of 1929 and the development of financial markets.

FEDERAL RESERVE BANK★

33 Liberty St. - www.ny.frb.org - guided tour (1hr) recommended booking approx. 1 month in advance- Mon-Fri at 1pm and 2pm except public holidays - arrive 30min before - valid ID essential - free. The austere facade as well as the railings on its windows and its sober lobby emphasize the importance of its function. It plays the hugely consequential role of establishing US monetary policy, and therefore influencing the world economy. The vault, buried more than 24m/79ft below street level, and 15m/49ft under sea level, houses billions of dollars of gold reserves belonging to the US and the central banks of approximately sixty countries; the contents constitute 25-30% of the world's reserves and it is the world's largest single reserve (more than 10 000t).

TRINITY CHURCH★

74 Trinity Place - www.trinitywall street.org - 7am-6pm - guided tour Mon-Fri at 2pm, Sun after mass from 11.15am - mobile app Trinity Wall Street Tour. Concerts on selected days, consult website for info.
Built in 1846, this was once the highest monument in New York. Its imposing neo-Gothic red sandstone facade was relatively unscathed by the collapse of the World Trade Center, despite being so close. The cemetery contains 17C tombs.

MUSEUM OF JEWISH HERITAGE★★

Ⓜ *line 1 (stations South Ferry or Rector Street), lines 4 and 5 (station Bowling Green) or line R (stations Whitehall Street or Rector Street. 36 Battery Place - ☎ 646 437 4202 - www.mjhnyc.org - daily except Sat 10am-6pm (Wed-Thur 8pm, Fri 5pm and 3pm Nov-March) - closed Thanksgiving and Jewish festivals - $12 (under 12s free); free Wed. 4pm-8pm. Allow 1hr.* The understated grace of the building and well-curated exhibits make this a fascinating museum of Jewish history. The six sides of the building and six-tiered roof are a tribute to the six million Jewish people who died in the Holocaust and the six points of the Star of David. The documents presented, including the particularly moving **Klarsfeld Pillars**, tell the story of the Holocaust, Jewish immigration to the US and the revival of Judaism. The café offers one of the finest views of the harbor.

SKYSCRAPER MUSEUM★

39 Battery Pl. - ☎ 212 968 1961 - www.skyscraper.org - daily except Mon-Tue 12pm-6pm - $5.
Exhibitions, models, photos and maps showcase New York's architectural heritage in an audacious and attractive celebration of the city's emblematic vertical lines.

21

STATUE OF LIBERTY★★★

Access to the pier where the boat departs by Ⓜ lines 4 and 5 (Bowling Green) or line R (Whitehall Street). A ferry departing from the adjacent pier at Castle Clinton (ticket office) serves the Statue of Liberty, then Ellis Island. Statue Cruises – ℘ 877 523 9849 - www.statuecruises.com - June-Sep : departures every 25min from 8.30am to 5pm (4pm in Sept.) ; rest of the year: dep. every 25min from 9.20am to 3.30pm - combined ticket for the Statue of Liberty and Ellis Island : statue pedestal $18.50 (4-12 years/ $9), statue crown (minimum 3 months advanced booking) $21.50 (4-12 years/$12) - incl. audio guide - free tours given by park rangers.

A symbol of the friendship between the US and France since the American Revolution, the Statue of Liberty remains one of the country's icons; Sculptor **Frédéric Auguste Bartholdi** chose liberty to symbolize entry into the New World and to signal to the world the importance of this principle. In 1884, the statue, financed and constructed in Paris by the French, was presented to the American ambassador, then deconstructed to be taken across the Atlantic.
The American funds collected thanks to the public solicitations of *New York World* publisher **Joseph Pulitzer** facilitated the construction of the pedestal. The statue reached New York in June 1885 and was inaugurated on October 28, 1886. The story goes that Bartholdi gave the statue the body of his wife and the face of his mother. He first made a plaster model, then enlisted **Gustave Eiffel** to construct an interior skeleton of iron and steel, weighing 125 tons. The architect covered it in 300 copper plates to create the statue's green "skin". Lady Liberty measures more than 45m/147ft from the base to the torch. A person could be clasped in its hand (4.8m/15.7ft-long) and its foot would easily crush any unfortunate soul. The gold-plated torch was replaced during a 1980s renovation.

ELLIS ISLAND★★ AND IMMIGRATION MUSEUM★★

www.nps.gov/elis. When you arrive, go straight to the desk to get your tickets for the film, as sessions fill up quickly. Ellis Island was chosen, in 1892 as the entrance point to the United States for immigrants from Europe. The Art Nouveau style building where they were registered now houses documents and artifacts relating the conditions and experiences of the millions of immigrants who passed through here; some were accepted, some pushed back, and all would have waited hours or even days. The center closed in 1954.

BATTERY PARK

Before the arrival of the Dutch (🕭 p. 152), the southern tip of Manhattan was covered in marshland. The strip that forms today's Battery Park and the piers was reclaimed from the sea. The park is named after the two artillery batteries installed there during the War of 1812.
The first is located on Governors

Ellis Island Immigration Museum

Island; the second, Castle Clinton (♿ below), occupied another islet 100m/328ft from the river bank. In 1870, the passage between the river bank and Castle Clinton was filled, creating the current arrangement of Battery Park. From the **promenade★**, you will see the Statue of Liberty, Ellis Island and the banks of New Jersey. Among the sculptures in the park, don't miss **Sphere★** (Fritz Koenig, 1971), which has become a memorial to the victims of September 11.

It was positioned on the central plaza of the World Trade Center before the attacks, and is set to return to its original place after the construction is completed.

Castle Clinton – ✆ 212 344 7220 - www.nps.gov/cacl - 7.45am-5pm, guided tours (30min) daily at 10am, 12pm, 2pm, 4pm - free. This small circular fort, which once housed an artillery battery, was converted in 1821 into an opera house and theater, the **Castle Garden**. It then served as a welcome center for new immigrants (1855-1890) before the construction of the site on Ellis Island. In 34 years, more than eight million people passed through its doors. From 1896 to 1941, it would house the New York City Aquarium.

Pier A★ – This is the oldest pier in Manhattan, a venerable Victorian-style structure, punctuated by a clock-tower. At the foot of Pier A, the **American Merchant Marine Memorial** pays homage to the shipwrecked of a boat torpedoed during the Second World War.

NATIONAL MUSEUM OF THE AMERICAN INDIAN★★

1 Bowling Green - www.american indian.si.edu - 10am-5pm (Thur 8pm) - free.
The museum, housed in the imposing customs building (1907) conceived by Cass Gilbert, features an elliptical rotunda adorned in frescoes by New York painter Reginald Marsh (1898-1954). Created in 1994 by the Smithsonian Institution, the museum is dedicated to the presentation and preservation of the culture of Native Americans, both historical and contemporary. The museum also organizes film projections, concerts and dance performances.

STATEN ISLAND FERRY★★

At the end of Whitehall St. - www. siferry.com - every 30min in the day, every 15min during rush hour (7am-9am and 5pm-7pm), once an hour at night between 1.30am and 5.30am - 25min crossing, allow 1hr30min for just the journey there and back - times are subject to variation, check online before your trip - pedestrians and bikes only - free.
Wrap up warm – it can get very cold out on the water! On the journey there, position yourself on the right to get a distant view of the Statue of Liberty. On the way back, head to the front of the ferry to see Manhattan coming into view. Around 20 million people use this ferry every year, of which most are commuters going to work. For tourists, it's a unique and free way to enjoy some stunning **views** of the city.

BATTERY MARITIME BUILDING★

*11 South St., at the end of Whitehall St.
- www.batterymaritimebuilding.com.*
This pretty Art Nouveau building
(1909) has been entirely restored,
with the original colors of its cast
iron facade brought back to life. Up
until 1938 the Brooklyn Ferry service
operated from the terminal. Today it
provides a summer ferry service to
Governors Island.

FRAUNCES TAVERN MUSEUM★

*54 Pearl St. - ☎ 212 425 1778 -
www.frauncestavernmuseum.org -
Mon-Fri 12pm-5pm, Sat-Sun 11am-5pm
- $7, 6-18 years $4 - free guided tours
Thursdays 1pm, Fri 2pm, Sat-Sun 1pm
and 2pm.*
This key site in the American
Revolution was originally the
residence of a rich merchant. It was
bought by Samuel Fraunces in 1762,
who turned it into a tavern. A group
who met here were the **Sons of
Liberty**, a clandestine organization
of American citizens at the end of the
18C who resisted British repression
during the rebellion of the Thirteen

Staten Island Ferry

25

Colonies against English rule. **George
Washington** would celebrate victory
over the English here. It was also the
site of many political meetings when
New York was the capital. It was
completely restored at the start of the
20C. Its rooms present documents on
the history of Independence.

Brooklyn Bridge in numbers

*For 20 years it was the longest suspension bridge in the world. Construction lasted 14
years and cost $25 million; 27 perished during its construction. The steel central span,
486m/1594ft long, is supported by two pylons which sink into the water of the East River,
41m/134ft below. The two archways culminate almost 48m/157ft above the deck of the
bridge. The main suspension cables are 40cm/15.7in thick. The pedestrian walkway, at
the top of the structure, was reconstructed between 1981 and 1983.*

SOUTH STREET SEAPORT HISTORIC DISTRICT★★

Situated to the south of Brooklyn Bridge, the **Port of New York**, founded in the 17C, was the first driver of the city's economy. Piers, warehouses and trading houses would gain influence as international commerce developed. The creation of a ferry line between Fulton Street and Brooklyn (1814), the opening of **Fulton Market** (1822) (the former fish market has been converted into a commercial and entertainment center), and the creation of the Erie Canal in 1825 would turn this into an area buzzing with activity. During the second half of the 19C, however, the **East River** would see maritime traffic decrease, with more going to the new piers in the deep waters of the **Hudson River**. It was only after 1967, when the area was designated a historic district, that the port slowly began to regain its appeal, offering a taste of the atmosphere of the beginning of New York.

SOUTH STREET SEAPORT MUSEUM★

12 Fulton St. - ℘ 212 748 8600 - www.southstreetseaportmuseum. org - Wed-Sun 11am-5pm to visit the exhibits on board the legendary boats (weather permitting)- $12, combined ticket with the Museum of City of New York. May-Oct: 2-hour cruises ($32).
The museum houses a significant collection of models, instruments and documents, as well as a collection of old ships along Piers 15 and 16, the most spectacular being 1885 cargo ship *Wavertree* and the 1907 Lightship *Ambrose.* The visit can be carried on to **Fulton Street★** and **Water Street★**, commercial streets restored to early 19C style, with some quaint old-fashioned shops.

BROOKLYN BRIDGE★★★

This is a testament to the technical prowess of the 19C. This iconic suspension bridge linking Manhattan to Brooklyn was inaugurated in May 1883. Before its construction, around 50 million people would take the ferry every year to cross the East River. Conceived by **John Augustus Roebling**, the architect of the suspension bridge over Niagara Falls, it was made by his son who drew inspiration from new European techniques. For the construction of its foundations, workers were submerged in wooden chambers pumped with compressed air, but the system lacked some refinement and many of them suffered from burst eardrums. The bridge is a masterpiece of aesthetics and engineering, featuring a central pedestrian walkway elevated above the traffic and neolithic granite archways amid vast network of cables. The **views** over Manhattan and the port are spectacular. Note that in nice weather, the pedestrian walkway can be very crowded. Watch out for cyclists.

Pier 15, South Street Seaport

Chinatown★★, Little Italy and Nolita

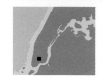

In bustling **Chinatown,** *sights and smells assail the senses. Of the infamous* **Little Italy,** *where once upon a time Mafia Godfathers dictated the law, only the prosciutto and parmesan remain.* **Nolita** *has become a super trendy extension of Soho.*

▶**Access:** Subway: Canal St., Spring St., Prince St., Grand St. and Broadway-Lafayette. Bus: M21, M55, M1.
Area maps p. 31 and 36. ***Detachable map BC7***.
▶**Tips:** Visit Chinatown in the morning when the streets are not yet too packed, then wander through Little Italy to Nolita, lively in the afternoons and evenings.

28

CHINATOWN★★

Chinese immigration to New York started in the 1870s. A decade later, this area was known for brothels, gambling houses and opium dens. Today, the Chinese population of Chinatown is 200 000, making it one of the largest such communities outside of Asia. Shops filled with gadgets are interspersed with tea sellers and purveyors of Eastern medicine, as well as a few trendy restaurants and cafés. On Canal St. are an abundance of designer imitations.
Museum of Chinese in America (MOCA) – *215 Centre St. (corner of Grand St.) - ℘ 212 619 4785 - www. mocanyc.org - daily except Mon 11am-6pm (Thur 9pm) - $ 10 (seniors and students $5, under 12s free).* This modern museum explores the ways of life of the Chinese diaspora in America.

LITTLE ITALY

The first Italian immigrants grouped together in this area which quickly became a hotbed of organized crime, controlled by the Mafia. Today, Little Italy has lost most of its Italians to other neighborhoods, but it's still a lovely area for a stroll. Box-set fans may happily recognize **Mulberry Street Café** *(no. 176)*, backdrop of much-loved series *The Sopranos.*

NOLITA

Cafés, little restaurants and trendy boutiques are sprinkled across the northern part of Little Italy's leafy streets (Nolita = "North of Little Italy"). **Old Saint Patrick's Cathedral**, in neo-Gothic style (1815), was until 1879 the Catholic cathedral of New York.

Tribeca★★ and Soho★★

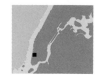

Tribeca *offers a happy mix of chic restaurants, warehouses converted into pricey lofts and art galleries. Beyond its luxury boutiques, charming delis and hyped bars,* **Soho** *is home to some of the most beautifully preserved cast iron architecture in the country. It was taken over by artists in the 1960s, and then inevitably became too expensive for the bohemians; today it's a haven for yuppies.*

▶**Access:** Subway Chambers St., Franklyn St. and Canal St. for Tribeca; Houston St., Broadway-Lafayette, Spring St. and Canal St. for Soho.
Area map p. 31. *Detachable map AB7*.
▶**Tip:** if you're an art lover, you will get a lot from wandering Tribeca, with the New York Gallery Guide in tow (www.artdealers.org/gallery-guide). Note that galleries are closed on Sundays and Mondays. If shopping is more your bag, head for Soho (boutiques open from 10am). There is much to please **architecture aficionados** in both areas.

TRIBECA★★

The name of the area comes from the contraction of **TRI**angle **BE**low **CA**nal, though technically it is more trapeze-shaped. At the start of the 18C, this section of town housed the residences of rich families. It was only in the middle of the 19C, when the quays of the Hudson River supplanted

South Street Seaport, that warehouses would fill the area. This was the great era of **cast-iron architecture** and brick; typically structures were built five or six floors high and housed offices or stockrooms. On the eve of the Second World War, this was one of the city's most industrious areas, bringing together manufacturing, services and trade. But during the

---

WHERE TO EAT	WHERE TO DRINK	SHOPPING	
Dean & Deluca.............. **5**	Eileen's Special Cheesecake.............**31**	Canal Street Market.....................**15**	Uniqlo............................**6**
Giorgione......................**12**	Houston Hall...............**21**	Nike................................**16**	NIGHTLIFE
Peking Duck House... **25**	Macao............................**23**	Philip Williams Posters.......................**3**	SOB's (Sound of Brazil).........**1**
Racines..........................**41**	Pegu Club.....................**27**	Prada..............................**5**	
Troquet..........................**48**	Smith & Mills...............**5**		

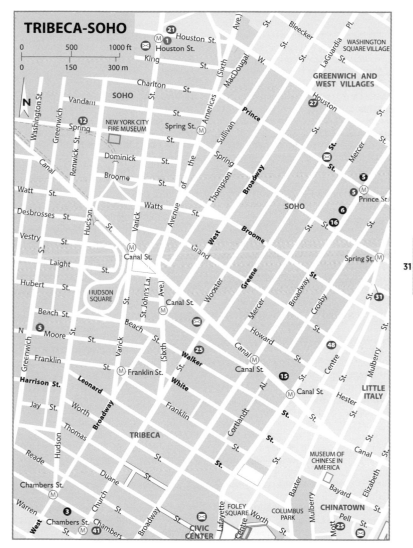

TRIBECA-SOHO

0   500   1000 ft

0   150   300 m

N

Houston St.
Houston St.
King St.

Charlton St.
SOHO
Vandam

Washington St.
Greenwich
Renwick
Spring

NEW YORK CITY FIRE MUSEUM

Dominick St.
Broome St.
Watt St.
Desbrosses St.
Vestry St.
Laight St.

Canal

Hudson

Varick

Hubert St.
Beach St.

Greenwich

Moore St.
Franklin
Harrison St.

Leonard
Jay St.
Broadway
Thomas
Worth

Hudson
Reade

Chambers St.
Warren
West
Chambers St.
Chambers

Church St.

HUDSON SQUARE

St. John's La.

Canal St.

(Sixth

Beach St.

Franklin St.

TRIBECA

Duane St.

Charlton St.
Spring St.
Avenue
the
of
Americas
Sullivan
Thompson

Prince
Broadway

Spring

Watts
West
Broome
Grand

Wooster
Greene
Mercer

Walker
White

Franklin

Canal St.

Howard

Mercer
Broadway
Crosby

Canal St.

WASHINGTON SQUARE VILLAGE

Bleecker St.
LaGuardia Pl.

GREENWICH AND WEST VILLAGES

Houston

Mercer
St.

SOHO

Prince St.

Spring St.

Canal St.

LITTLE ITALY

Hester St.

Mulberry

Centre St.
Cortlandt
St.

St.

St.

Lafayette
Worth

CIVIC CENTER

Broadway

FOLEY SQUARE

COLUMBUS PARK

Baxter
Bayard

MUSEUM OF CHINESE IN AMERICA

Canal

Mulberry
Mott
Pell

CHINATOWN

Elizabeth
St.

Centre

31

1960s, Tribeca saw a slow and painful fall in desirability, triggered by the decline in manufacturing and of the port. In 1970, Tribeca and its worn-out buildings were home to only 243 inhabitants.

The area was saved by the large number of artists pushed out of Soho by rocketing prices; creative types emigrated here and converted the warehouses and workshops into art galleries. Today, with a population of more than 10,000, including a number of celebrities (Robert De Niro, in particular, is known for his investment in the life of Tribeca), this neighborhood has become highly desirable once more. As you explore the area, be sure to pass by **Washington Market Park**, which was once one of the most active markets in New York. **Harrison Street**, a row of houses in Federal style, built between 1796 and 1828, gives an idea of what Tribeca would have looked like at this time. On **Leonard Street**, you'll find a number of imposing buildings such as the Clock Tower Building (headquarters of the New York Life Insurance Company) which features the last active mechanical clock in the city. Between **West Broadway** and Broadway you'll find the typical urban architecture of the 19C, with its brick facades in varying colors and its sets of cast iron columns. **White Street** is a fine example. **Tribeca Synagogue** is recognizable by its distinctive curved shape. On **Walker Street** you'll find various galleries and artists' studios. To the west, the **AT & T Headquarters Building** is an example of the popular New York Art Deco style. Built in 1918,

it features a spectacular lobby with stunning mosaics.

The area's latest icon, **56 Leonard Street,** designed by Swiss architects Herzog & de Meuron, stuns with its original design, resembling a number of irregular sized boxes stacked on top of each other.

In the last fifteen years, under the patronage of Robert De Niro, Tribeca has become the epicenter of New York cinema. In 2002, the actor created the **Tribeca Film Festival** with film producer Jane Rosenthal. The thinking was that New York deserved a noteworthy festival and that it would help breathe new life into the area, which was badly affected by September 11 attacks. The festival is not short on quality films and attendees; a selection of the world's best films are projected in various theaters across the area.

SOHO★★

Soho (**SO**uth of **HO**uston St) is one of the chicest areas in New York, with its boutiques, restaurants and art galleries. The neighborhood's history is quite varied.

In 1644, this area was home to Manhattan's first black community, a group of freed slaves. At the start of the 19C, wealthy bourgeois like James Fenimore Cooper, author of *The Last of the Mohicans*, began moving into the area.

Situated between the business-orientated Lower Manhattan in the south, and the large, elegant mansions of the north, Soho became one of the most densely populated

Soho

parts of town. Theaters, hotels, restaurants, casinos and shops were opened along **Broadway** and the surrounding streets. To please revelers, **Mercer Street** became a hub for brothels , with two thirds of New York's sex workers here at one point. Displeased by its evolution, the bourgeois eventually left Soho for the neighborhoods farther north, while the most prosperous commerces would move up to 5th Avenue. During the second half of the 19C, residences were slowly replaced by businesses, offices and warehouses. Architects began to employ a new construction technique: **cast iron architecture**. Developed by the English at the end of the 18C, it allowed for rapid construction and a range of new architectural styles. The lighter facades featured more windows. The cast iron elements, created in molds and reproduced in large quantity, could be combined in different combinations, according to the size of the building and demands of the client. The final construction was then painted. The result was whole streets lined with graceful colonnades, elegant cornicing and delicate pastel-painted pediments. Today, of the 400 cast irons in New York, around 300 can be found in Soho.

In the 20C, Soho became progressively neglected before being readopted by artist types, drawn by the huge lofts and vast, vacant warehouse spaces. There was an animated campaign to save the area's facades, and in 1973 Soho was classified as a historic district, after which it became the center of contemporary art in New York, attracting artists and new galleries. Prices subsequently sky-rocketed, causing an exodus of artists and galleries to Chelsea. The creative, vibrant and bohemian feel of the neighborhood made way for the strings of high-end boutiques you see today.

Broadway – In this part of town, Broadway is not associated with theaters, but rather is a hub for commerce and shopping. Note the stunning **Silk Exchange Building** (1895) at *487 Broadway*. The finely constructed building features an Italianized Rococo facade. On the northwest corner of Prince Street, **the Prada building** (no. 575) sets the tone: from 1991-2001 the site of the Guggenheim Soho, it now features elegant décor designed by architect Rem Koolhaas (**⚭** *Prada, p. 119*). The inauguration of the twelve-floor **Little Singer Building** (nos. 561-563), designed by Ernest Flagg in 1903, with its typically Beaux-Arts style heralded a new era for skyscrapers. It is easily recognizable by its lacy wrought iron floral motifs and long windows The **E.V. Haughwout Building** (nos. 488-492), considered in its time (1857) a veritable "Venetian palace", with its arcades, balustrades and Corinthian columns, was the city's first building with a cast iron facade and the first to have an elevator, installed by Elisha G. Otis.

Greene Street★ – You'll find the largest grouping of cast iron facades on this street, located west of Broadway. The two most interesting structures, designed by Isaac F. Duckworth in 1872 in Second Empire style, are nicknamed the **King and Queen of Greene Street** (nos. 72-76 and 28-30); the former features a grand porch supported by high columns and the latter a mansard roof with elaborate dormer windows.

Prince Street – Peppered with boutiques and art galleries, Prince Street houses a cast iron edifice featuring a *trompe-l'œil* brick wall facade: the work was created by the painter Richard Haas in 1975.

Broome Street – On the corner of Greene Street you'll find the **Gunther Building** (nos. 469-475), a beautiful wrought iron creation from 1873; see also the elegant building at *no. 448*.

West Broadway – Contemporary art and luxury boutiques (Armani, Elie Tahari, Dolce & Gabbana) occupy West Broadway.

Lower East Side★

Sunday morning is the best time to come and wander here, perusing the tempting shops selling everything from delicious, crusty bagels to bohemian blouses. The Lower East Side (LES) was the entry point for immigrants to New York, who lived crammed together in tenement buildings. The area has retained a touch of its former shabby look, but the murky buildings covered in graffiti belie the now-pricey area's incarnation as an ultra-hip district day and night. The bars, clubs and restaurants of the area blend chic, modern décor and natty knick-knacks. In the small hours, revelers dance to blues, rock and electro.

▶**Access:** Subway: Delancey Street, Essex Street, Grand Street, 2nd Avenue. *Area map p. 36. Detachable map BC7*.

▶**Tip:** Head to the Lower East Side on a Sunday. Start with brunch, and then wander on Orchard Street (shops closed until 10-11am). This is a great area for dinner. New bars and restaurants open constantly. Pick somewhere that looks interesting and is full, and give it a go. Avoid Saturdays (the Sabbath) as some businesses may be closed.

In the late 19C and early 20C, the Lower East Side, inexpensive and diverse, was the area of new arrivals, a sort of holding room between their country of origin and vast New York. At one time, the Lower East Side was the most densely populated zone in the world. From 1820, communities of freed **blacks** and **Irish** grouped together in the area, as well as a significant **Chinese community**, working on the construction of railroads. Chased out of their country by famine after 1840, the **Irish** arrived in the hundreds of millions during the 19C, joined by **Germans** fleeing war and religious persecution. The first wave of **Jewish immigration**, from Germany, was followed by the arrival of Jews from Russia and Poland who were fleeing pogroms. **Italians** came across in the second half of the 19C, settling near the Irish and founding Little Italy. Finally **Puerto Ricans** would move in to the area at the end of the 19C and during the first half of the 20C. Though there is still a small Jewish community here, evidenced by the synagogues and a few shops and restaurants, the last immigrant populations still living here are principally Latinos and people of Asian origin. Today, LES is increasingly losing its idiosyncratic character, as it has become one of the trendiest going-out spots for the young, hip crowd. However, there are still traces of its history: though many buildings have been razed, some streets still retain a

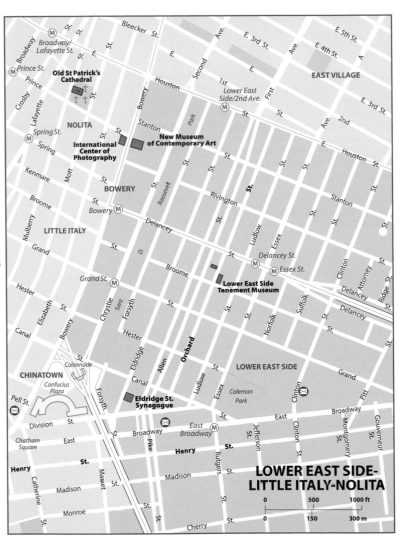

36

Bleecker St.

Broadway/Lafayette St. Ⓜ

Broadway

Prince St. Ⓜ

Old St Patrick's Cathedral

Prince

Crosby

Lafayette

NOLITA

Spring St. Ⓜ

Spring

International Center of Photography

Kenmare

Mott

Broome

BOWERY

Bowery Ⓜ

Mulberry

LITTLE ITALY

Grand

Hester

Grand St. Ⓜ

Elizabeth

Canal

Bowery

Chrystie

Sara

Forsyth

Hester

Eldridge

Allen

Orchard

CHINATOWN

Colonnade

Confucius Plaza

Pell St. ⊠

Division St.

Chatham Square

East

Henry

Catherine

Madison

Monroe

Bowery

Houston

Stanton

Park

New Museum of Contemporary Art

Roosevelt

Rivington

Delancey

Broome

Ludlow

Essex

Delancey St. Ⓜ

Essex St. Ⓜ

Lower East Side Tenement Museum

Norfolk

Suffolk

LOWER EAST SIDE

Ludlow

Essex

Coleman Park

Eldridge St. Synagogue

Forsyth

Pike

Broadway

⊠ East Broadway Ⓜ

Henry

Rutgers

Jefferson

Madison

Clinton

East

Broadway

Montgomery

Gouverneur

Clinton

Attorney

Ridge St.

Delancey

Stanton

Houston St.

E. 5th St.

Ave.

E. 4th St.

E. 3rd St.

Ave.

EAST VILLAGE

E. 3rd St.

Lower East Side/2nd Ave. Ⓜ

Second

First

Ave. 2nd

Pitt

Grand

Clinton

Cherry

LOWER EAST SIDE-LITTLE ITALY-NOLITA

0   500   1000 ft

0   150   300 m

Couture and cigars

The garment making business of New York began in the Lower East Side, where young women worked in their homes. The cheap cost and ready availability of labor then lead to the establishment of shared workshops. This area also produced cigars in an industry that was directed by Puerto Ricans, with many immigrants from the Caribbean working here.

bit of the atmosphere of a bygone New York, with old-fashioned shops and cafés and the distinctive brick buildings with narrow windows and iron fire escapes. Their future is not assured, however, as prices continue to skyrocket, and new restaurants and luxury hotels open constantly, attracting an ever-more wealthy clientèle. Nevertheless, you can still discover some authentic charm by wandering **Ludlow Street**★ and **Orchard Street**, stopping for a snack in one of the Jewish delis along the way.

The southern part of Orchard Street is occupied by shops selling cheap clothes and leather luggage, some inexpensive tailors and a few upholsters' and decorators' workshops; the northern part is dominated by chic boutiques and restaurants. Every Sunday, the road is closed to traffic for an open-air market, which charms with its relaxed, timeless ambiance.

NEW MUSEUM OF CONTEMPORARY ART★

235 Bowery - ℘ 212 219 1222 - www.newmuseum.org - daily except Mon and Tue 11am-6pm; Thur 9pm - $18, pay what you wish Thur - 7-9pm.

Small gift shop and pleasant café on the ground floor
Japanese architects Kazuyo Sejima and Ryue Nishizawa/ SANAA designed an accumulation of zinc cubes that seem to only just be balancing, maybe as if to demonstrate the unstable nature of contemporary art. The museum houses collections oriented towards new media, spanning digital pop art and installations.

INTERNATIONAL CENTER OF PHOTOGRAPHY

℘ 212 857 0000 - www.icp.org - daily except Mon 10am-6pm (until 9pm Thur) - $ 14, free under 14s.
Founded by Robert Capa in 1974, the centre, formerly located in Midtown West *(1113 Ave of Americas)* now has a new home. Since June 2016, it has been in the premises of 250 Bowery, where you will discover temporary exhibitions dedicated to photojournalism.

LOWER EAST SIDE TENEMENT MUSEUM★★

108 Orchard St. - ℘ 212 982 8420 - www.tenement.org - guided tour only (leaving from Museum Shop):

10.30am-6.30pm (visiting hours vary, consult the website) - $25. Free film, at the back of the shop (10am-6.30pm, until 8.30pm Thur). Number of visitors limited; book online or on ☎ 877 975 3786.

Between 1863 and 1935, 7 000 people lived in the same **tenement building** at 97 Orchard Street. The cramped, overcrowded apartments were generally sparsely or poorly furnished. The exhibits present the homes of different families with the rooms preserved in their original state. Personal artifacts and documents tell the stories of the people who lived here : Jews fleeing Europe, clandestine Catholic Sicilian immigrants, and Irish people forced to leave by the famine.

The stories of poor and cramped living conditions, troubles and struggle form a moving backdrop to the exhibits. A film which draws from original documents and interviews from the period evokes the day-to-day life of immigrants who were often lost in a country where they barely spoke the language.

HENRY STREET

This quiet street was the heart of the first Jewish quarter. Here you will find some interesting architectural vestiges from the end of the 19C. Founded in 1893, the **Henry Street Settlement** *(no. 263)* occupied a group of renovated brick houses. It was here that Lillian Wald founded a sort of community center (the Settlement), providing poor inhabitants of the area with care, financial aid and social services. A Settlement took the form of a small building occupied in general by women working as nurses, teachers and social workers, helping disadvantaged people; these centers ensured the maintenance of a minimum of social integration in troubled areas. At this time, half of all Manhattan's Settlements could be found in the Lower East Side.

MANHATTAN BRIDGE

C8 Open to *pedestrians (south side) and cyclists (north side)*.
Where LES meets Chinatown is this metal bridge linking Lower

Lower East Side Tenement Museum

© S. Raccanello/Sime/ Photononstop

38

© Ph. Renault/~emis.fr

Manhattan Bridge seen from Dumbo

Manhattan to Dumbo (down under the Manhattan-Brooklyn overpass) in Brooklyn. Constructed in 1912, it was the fourth to be built on the East River (after Brooklyn Bridge, Williamsburg Bridge and Queensboro Bridge). After an initial project proposal featuring towers crowned with minarets, which was rejected, a second design using an innovative suspension system, employing chains rather than twisted cables, was suggested, before also being rejected. The project that was finally adopted retained only the towers, with a slightly lighter aspect than those of Brooklyn Bridge.
For a fine view of the bridge and a great photo, go to Washington St on the Brooklyn side, in Dumbo (*see photo above.*)

Greenwich Village★★

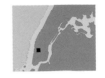

Greenwich Village is known for being the spiritual home of writers, artists and dissenters and a center for jazz and blues. This was once the place of intellectuals in New York, and also the favored area of the Beat Generation and hippies. Today, it's full of celebrities, the bourgeoisie and students who attend the nearby universities. Explore the area in spring time when the white blossoms of the Japanese plum tress fall to the street and café tables spill out onto the sidewalk. Expect a bohemian atmosphere – and possibly some celebrity sightings

▶**Access:** Subway: West 4th St., Christopher St., 8th St.-NYU. Bus: M8, M11, M14A, M14D, M20, M21, M55.
Area map p. 41. *Detachable map AB6*.
▶**Tip:** Visit Washington Square on the weekend to see performances by street artists. In the evening head to Bleecker Street to catch some jazz.

40

When New Yorkers speak about "the **Village**", they generally refer to the West – or Greenwich – Village. In 1696, the English founded the village of Greenwich. During the 18C, rich property owners lay claim to the area, but it retained its bucolic charm. The start of the 19C brought change: the establishment of 5th Avenue to the north and the development of the docks and factories along the Hudson. Bourgeois residents were replaced by new immigrants, and writers, artists and activists. At the turn of the 20C,

the Village had become a hub for the American avant-garde. Clubs and cafés served as the setting for lively meetings among political radicals, poets and painters. In 1913 **The Eight** (⭐ *p. 160*) organized the Armory Show; the 1920s and 1930s were the age of New York jazz. The 1940s saw the birth of abstract expressionist painting; the 50s was the era of the Beat generation and the 60s saw the explosion of the folk music scene. The tolerant atmosphere meant that a gay community also developed

WHERE TO EAT			
Ancolie	⓸	Spotted Pig	㉛
Corner Bistro	⓽	Umami Burger	㊸
Frankies Spuntino	㉜		
Mary's Fish Camp	㉞		

WHERE TO DRINK	
Caffe Vivaldi	⑨
Magnolia Bakery	⑧

The Top of the Standard	㊱
SHOPPING	
C.O. Bigelow	❿
Murray's	㊱
Uncle Sam's Army Navy Outfitters	⑫

Urban Outfitters	⓫
NIGHTLIFE	
Café Wha?	㉒
Cielo	⑱
Village Underground	❺
55 Bar	❹

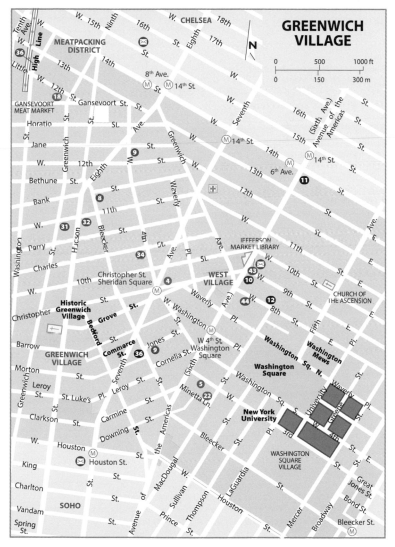

41

here, though not without struggle. In **Christopher Park**, you'll see statues (same-sex male and same-sex female couples) by George Segal (1924-2000). Opposite, at 53 Christopher St. is **Stonewall Inn**, the first gay bar of the area. A national monument, this is where the annual Pride parade finishes. It's famous for the violent clashes between the LGBTQ community and police that took place here in 1969, the catalyst for the gay rights movement in the US.

WASHINGTON SQUARE★

A popular spot surrounded by **New York University**, this park opens onto 5th Avenue with a Beaux-Arts style triumphal arch, finished in 1892. To the south, the impressive fountain is the backdrop for street artists. On the south side, you'll find serious players gathered round the outdoor chess boards. Over the years, Washington Square has become a place to relax, a picnic spot and a site for all manner of protest. The area around this park has always been a haunt for intellectuals. **Washington Square North**, with its elegant neo-Greek buildings, has been the address of many great writers (Henry James, Edith Wharton, John Dos Passos).

Painters Edward Hopper and Jackson Pollock, the poet Edwin Arlington Robinson and the sculptor Gertrude Vanderbilt Whitney (founder of the Whitney Museum) lived in **Washington Mews**. This little road was once the site of stables and servants' quarters. Here you'll find an idiosyncratic charm, not matched anywhere else in New York: expect whitewashed houses, climbing ivy and bucolic cobblestone.

42

Greenwich Village gems

At 56 7th Ave. S, you'll find **Greenwich Locksmiths**, *immediately recognizable by its amazing facade covered in keys (with a matching chair by the front door). The artwork has turned owner Philip Mortillaro into a local celebrity!*

*If you watched the series Friends, you'll likely recognize the corner of Grove and Bedford Sts., which **featured as the outside shot in every episode**. The main characters lived in Greenwich Village, but the series was actually filmed in a studio in Burbank, California. This building was chosen because it was the apartment building of one of the show's creators.*

*At 17 Grove St. is a white **house with red shutters** (1822), one of the few remaining wooden houses in the area.*

*At 75 1/2 Bedford St. is another curiosity: **the narrowest house in the city**, measuring only 2.9m/9.5ft across (and 9m/29ft deep)!*

*Finally, be sure to have a peek at **Dominique Ansel Bakery**, (189 Spring St.). Ansel invented the "cronut", a cross between a croissant and a doughnut. New Yorkers adore them and many arrive at the crack of dawn to wait in line to buy them, although now you can order at nyc.cronutpreorder.com. Only 350 are produced each day. $ 6 each.*

St. Luke's Place, Greenwich Village

HISTORIC GREENWICH VILLAGE★★

To the east of 6th Avenue lies the oldest part of Greenwich Village, reminiscent of what the Village would have been like at the start of the 20C, with its tree-lined roads, red brick houses and signature brownstones. On **Grove Street** are Federal-style houses, like those in verdant Grove Court (nos. 10-12). The oldest, dating from 1799 stands on **Bedford Street** (no. 77). At 17 Grove St., on the **northeast corner of Grove and Bedford Sts**, you'll find a three-floor wooden house, a rare sight in New York. 102 Bedford St .is also well worth a look: here you'll find an extravagant 1925 house that looks straight out of a Bavarian village. This area is packed with significant historical sites from the world of literature and theater. On Bedford Street, watering hole **Chumley's** (no. 86) was frequented by the likes of Steinbeck, Willa Cather and Edna St. Vincent Millay, though note that today it's restaurant unlike the original bar. On Commerce St., **Cherry Lane Theater** (no. 38), founded in the 1920s, is one of the most innovative in New York. Don't miss the quirky Twin Sisters (nos. 39 and 41), two brick houses built in 1832; according to the legend, they were built by a sailor whose two daughters were incapable of living under the same roof.

East Village★

The East Village has quite a varied history. In the 15C, much of the area was farm. In the early 19C, handsome townhouses were built. Mid 19C saw an influx of Irish and German immigrants, then Poles and Ukrainians. In the 1950s and 60s, Beatniks, artists, musicians, and hippies moved in, followed by a strong punk and goth scene. In the 1980s, the neighborhood was the center of cool, with all-night clubs, bars, and music venues, but it was also marred by drugs, and many of the buildings were in disrepair. Today, the East Village is ultra-trendy and its real estate expensive, but its tree-lined side streets remain fairly serene.

▶**Access:** Subway: Astor Place, 1st Avenue, 2nd Avenue. Bus: M1, M2, M3, M8, M14A, M14D, M15, M102. ***Detachable map C6-7***.
▶**Tip:** Pair your visit to the East Village with Greenwich Village or LES.

COOPER UNION FOUNDATION BUILDING★

44 *C6* Built in 1859 by a self-made industrialist, this neo-Roman building is the oldest steel frame building in the city. It houses a prestigious university. In 2009, it was expanded with the curved building situated at **41 Cooper Square★**.

MERCHANT'S HOUSE MUSEUM★

BC6-7 29 East 4th St. - 𝄢 212 777 1089 - www.merchantshouse.org - daily except Tue-Wed 12pm-5pm (Thur 8pm) - tour (1hr) at 2pm, also 6.30pm on Thur - $ 15 (under 12s free). With period furnishings, this brick Federal style house shows how a rich trader and family would have lived in the 19C.

ST MARK'S PLACE★

C6-7 The tattoo parlors and fashionable cafés hint just lightly at this street's long-gone anarchist past.

TOMPKINS SQUARE PARK★

C7 Planted with hundred-year-old elms, this 10.5-acre (4ha) park has served as the rallying point for all manner of dissenters over the years, from socialists at the start of the 20C to Vietnam War protesters.

ST MARK'S-IN-THE-BOWERY

C6 131 East 10th St - stmarksbowery.org. This neo-Greek style church (1799), replaced the chapel of Stuyvesant (👍 p. 150), buried in the adjoining cemetery.

RENWICK TRIANGLE★

C6 On the corner of 10th St and Stuyvesant St you'll find 16 Italian style residences in brick and sandstone, created by **James Renwick**.

Chelsea★★ *and Meatpacking District*★

Chelsea's main avenues are firmly 21C, but its leafy side streets, lined in red brick townhouses, are practically unchanged since the 19C. In far east Chelsea, many former warehouses have been converted into excellent free art galleries Further south, arty and sometimes snobby Meatpacking attracts slick, dressed-up New Yorkers who patronize its restaurants and clubs. Renzo Piano's sleek Whitney Museum has brought substantial culture to the area.

▶**Access:** Subway: 14th, 23rd, 28th Sts. Bus: M8, M11, M12, M14A, M14D, M20, M23
Area map p. 41. ***Detachable map AB5-6***.
▶**Tip:** Start your morning with a trip to Chelsea Market, then head north, to arrive at the galleries when they open at 11am (closed Sunday and Monday), before exploring the High Line (good for a picnic). Shoppers can opt instead to hit 6th Avenue (Avenue of the Americas), where all the big brands and a clutch of discount stores can be found. Keep the fun going into the night in the clubs of Meatpacking.

CHELSEA MARKET★

B6 */5 9th Ave. (between 15th and 16th Sts.) - Mon-Sat 7am-9pm, Sun 8am-8pm.* Thanks to careful restoration, you can sill see the structural vestiges of the Nabisco biscuit factory (1898) that this trendy food market once was. There are many places to eat here but not a lot of seating. In nice weather, eat on the High Line or along the Hudson River.

CHELSEA HISTORIC DISTRICT★

B5 Of the old English Chelsea, there remain just a few quiet roads, lined with tall houses decked in climbing vines and wisteria. The main concentration of these can be found between 9th and 10th Avenues, along 20th, 21st and 22nd Streets. The best-preserved buildings can be found on **Cushman Row**★ *(406-418 West 20th St.)*. High stone staircases lead up to the red brick of the neo-Greek facades, decorated out front with matching little gardens, hemmed in by wrought iron railings.

GALLERY DISTRICT★★

B5 The largest concentration of galleries can be found to the west of 10th Avenue. Start in the south by 20th St and head north until you

© Peter Wrenn/Michelin

Cushman Row, Chelsea Historic District

Dedicated to the art of Tibet, Nepal and Bhutan (Himalaya), this museum brings together paintings, sculptures, textiles and sacred objects reflecting more than two thousand years of the cultures of these peoples. Their spirituality, approach to the world and the sophistication of their artisans are displayed elegantly in warm-toned rooms (yellow, purple). You will periodically hear incantations played, giving the experience an almost mystical dimension.

MEATPACKING DISTRICT★

B5-6 To the north of Greenwich Village is the Meatpacking district, which was the most significant center of beef production in the country in the middle of the 19C. With the development of transport, the abattoirs moved closer to the farming districts, leaving only Gansevoort Meat Market wholesale market. During the 1990s, this area had a somewhat shady reputation, but for the past two decades, its cobbled streets and vast warehouses have attracted a fashionable crowd, making this a hip district packed with cool clubs and fashion designers.

reach 27th St. At 529 W. 20th St, is a five-story building housing some 30 galleries. Don't be put off by the somewhat unappealing aspect of the entrance hall: the galleries of 24th St are known for the quality of their exhibitions (visit Mary Boone Gallery, Luhring Augustine, Metro Pictures). The works, of varying styles, offer a fairly exhaustive cross-section of contemporary art.

RUBIN MUSEUM OF ART★★

B6 *150 West 17th St. - ℘ 212 620 5000 - www.rubinmuseum.org - daily except Tue 11am-5pm (Wed 9pm, Fri 10pm, Sat-Sun 6pm) - $15 (under 12s free); Fri 6pm-10pm free*

WHITNEY MUSEUM OF AMERICAN ART★★

A6 *99 Gansevoort St. - ℘ 212 570 3600 - www.whitney.org - Sun-Mon & Wed 10.30am-6pm, Fri-Sat 10am-10pm - closed Tues (except Jul-Aug) - $25 (seniors and students $18, pay what you wish Fri 7-10pm).*

The Whitney was founded in 1931 in Greenwich Village by the artist-collector Gertrude Vanderbilt Whitney. In 2015 it left its location on Museum Mile for this space, designed by Renzo Piano. The bright, modular exhibition spaces are impressive, with floor-to-ceiling windows offering views over the Hudson River and the east of Manhattan. Each floor has a beautiful terrace with a panoramic view over the High Line.

The collection centers around American art from the 20C and 21C, with a collection comprising 23000 works by more than 3000 American artists (including 3000 paintings and drawings by **Edward Hopper** alone). Only a small part of the collection is on display at any one time, with much of the space dedicated to **temporary exhibitions**, which place American art in the context of global art movements past and present.

Visitors will be taken through the beginnings of **modern American art,** with its influences from European movements—the colors of Fauvism and the geometric shapes of Cubism. Artists in the collection include Marsden Hartley, Peggy Bacon, Oscar Bluemner, Max Weber, Georgia O'Keeffe, Charles Sheeler, Stuart Davis, Arshile Gorky and Milton Avery. The collection spans the urban realism of the early 20C and more abstract geometric painting before coming to the realism of the 1930s. Though the uncontested star of the museum is Edward Hopper, you'll also find Paul Cadmus and Reginald Marsh. Next come the abstract expressionists, Robert Motherwell and Clyfford Still, Alexander Calder, and Franz Kline; contemporary artists like Andy Warhol, Kara Walker and Yayoi Kusama; and the more recent Kiki Smith.

HIGH LINE★★

A6 www.thehighline.org
Running parallel to the Hudson, this abandoned railway line once served to transport goods for the industrialized part Manhattan's west side. The elevated section linking Gansevoort Market to 34th Street, around Chelsea and Penn Station, has been transformed into a **raised green belt**. The path starts in Meatpacking and snakes through the buildings of Chelsea and up to lower Midtown. The first section, from 14th to 20th Sts., was inaugurated in June 2009. In less than a year, it had already welcomed more than 2m visitors. The smart design facilitates a slick juxtaposition of some of the original rails with contemporary architecture, all set off by tall grasses and flowers; you'll find benches and sun loungers, great spots for watching the sun set over the Hudson in the evening.

The last section, between 30th and 34th St, opened in 2014. Along the route are several extraordinary buildings to look out for, such as the **IAC Building** (Frank Gehry), **100 11th Avenue** (Jean Nouvel) and **HL23** residence (Neil Denari). Take in the panoramic vista at the secluded viewpoint above 23rd Street.

47

Hudson Yards, the new face of New York

*Between 30th and 34th Sts., from the Hudson to 10th Ave, a forest of cranes announces the largest private real estate project in the history of the country. Across 1.2 million m²/12.9mft² in the heart of Manhattan, Hudson Yards will comprise a clutch of skyscrapers housing offices, hotels, apartments, shopping centers and restaurants, as well as a huge public park. The first spaces opened 2018, and the last stone of the **gargantuan building site** is expected to be placed in 2025. Hudson Yards is being framed by its developers as the new epicenter of Manhattan, and will cost around $20 billion. To attract visitors, the development is going for outrageous scale and ambition, encapsulated in two of the most unusual developments of the project. In 2019, a **suspended terrace** will open on the side of a glass skyscraper; its surface will measure 465 m2/5005ft2 and will stand 335 m/1099ft high, making it the highest observation point in the city. "The Vessel," a giant knot of staircases leading nowhere and shaped like a bees nest and is perhaps even more astounding. This 15-storey structure will contain 154 interconnected flights of stairs, taking in 2500 steps. It's expected to open in 2019.*

48

HUDSON RIVER PARK ★

B4 A5-7 *www.hudsonriverpark.org*
This is another path along the Hudson. Where the High Line offers urban environs, Hudson River Park provides a different perspective: secluded from the tumult of the city.

From 59th St to **Battery Park**, you'll see cyclists, strollers, day-dreamers and joggers who come here for the protected bike and walking lanes, a cool breeze from th river, green spaces and welcoming park benches. A great spot for taking in a different, more relaxing side of New York.

Along the route, little marinas housing **cruise boats** offer trips on the Hudson and in the bay. Circle Line Cruises *(Pier 83, 42nd St at 12th Ave)* has a good reputation.

Chelsea Piers *(Pier 62 - between 17th and 23rd Sts. - ☎ 212 336 6777 - www. chelseapiers.com -* ✖ *-* 🅿 *$12/hr)* is a huge complex encompassing four piers and various sports clubs (skating, swimming, bowling, etc.) On Pier 62, children will also enjoy the pretty **carousel** on the edge of the river. Cyclists can rent **bikes** by 44th St. or use Citibike (many docks along and just opposite the path).

Union Square and Madison Square★

With Chelsea, this collection of neighborhoods links Downtown and Midtown. The west portion is home to big-name shops, public squares and beautiful cast iron buildings, including the legendary Flatiron Building. Residential areas stretch out on the east side.

▶**Access:** Subway: Union Square, 14th, 23rd, 28th Sts. *Detachable map C6*.
▶**Tip:** Visit on Mondays, Wednesdays, Fridays and Saturdays, when the Union Square farmers' market is on.

UNION SQUARE PARK

Created in 1831, this park has long been the site of various protests, but it's also a place to sit in the shade. Around the square are some of the first skyscrapers of New York. A **farmers' market** is held here Mon, Wed, Fri, and Sat, with stalls selling dairy products, flowers, fruits and veg, and baked goods; the emphasis is on organic products, and all are produced in New York and the surrounding states (Pennsylvania, New Jersey, etc.). Union Square attracts aspiring artists and street musicians, as well as busy workers who stop to eat sandwiches on their lunch breaks. Little metal tables and chairs are set up on the northern side of the park, across from one of the playgrounds.

GRAMERCY PARK★

Surrounded by beautiful houses but, alas, reserved only for those who live on the park. It is one of just two private parks in New York (the other is in Sunnyside, Queens).

FLATIRON BUILDING★★

This legendary building was New York's first skyscraper (1902) and, at the time, the world's highest building of its kind (87m/285ft). Its 21 floors, supported by a cast iron structure, Italian Beaux-Arts style and idiosyncratic shape are the work of **Daniel Burnham**. Its stunningly narrow iron-like shape (hence the name), occupies a triangle between Broadway, 5th Avenue and 22nd Street.

THEODORE ROOSEVELT'S BIRTHPLACE

28 East 20th St. - ℘ 212 260 1616 - www.nps.gov/thrb - daily except Sun & Mon 9am-5pm - free.
The house in which the 26th president of the United-States (1901-1909) was born was constructed in 1848 and

5th Avenue by Madison Square

© espiegle/iStockphoto.comphoto.com

destroyed in 1916. The present-day building (1920) presents a collection of objects belonging to the president and his family.

MADISON SQUARE★

This is a lovely place to take a break. The square was once the central point of an upscale district and served as the terrain for the city's first baseball club. A few blocks away, at 4 Pennsylvania Plaza, sits the immense venue **Madison Square Garden**, site of concerts and basketball games (home of the New York Knicks).

MUSEUM OF SEX★

C5-6 *233 5th Ave. - ℘212 689 6337 - www.museumofsex.com - 10am-9pm (Fri-Sat 11pm), last entrance 1hr before - $20.50 (+ taxes) - under 18s not admitted.*

This museum traces the history of the pornography industry in New York, from the first pin-ups of the 19C to pornographic films and magazines sex toys and erotic posters. You'll find a number of themed exhibits, some playful and funny – all of them very explicit!

Midtown West★★★ *and the Theater District*

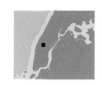

Everything about Midtown is larger than life. Here, you'll find glass and steel skyscrapers, the giant neon signs of Times Square, the theaters of Broadway, the flagship stores of 5th Avenue, magical views from the Empire State Building and Rockefeller Center, and the fabulous modern and contemporary art collection at MoMA. All in all, it's enough to make you dizzy, but in the best possible way.

▶**Access:** Subway: Bryant Park, 5th Avenue, Times Sq.-42nd St, 34th St.-Herald Sq, 34th St.-Penn Station, 49th St, Rockefeller Ctr. Bus: M1, M2, M3, M4, M5, M7, M42, M55, M104.
Detachable map C4-5.
▶**Tip:** MoMA is free every Friday after 4pm. If you want to go to the top of the Empire State Building, allow at least 1hr for waiting in line.

51

BROADWAY★
THEATER DISTRICT

When New York was created, today's Midtown was just a patch of uneven countryside. But while immigration brought poor populations to the south of the city, those who made their fortune would settle further north, along 5th Avenue, followed in turn by department stores and chic hotels. This fine set needed entertaining and so the **Theater District** was born, with the opening in 1895 of the Olympia. In little time, almost 80 theaters would spring up on Broadway from 6th to 8th Avenues, between 40th and 57th Streets, around what became **Times Square**★★. Originally created for light entertainment and revues, these addresses would go on to stage the works of great American playwrights, then musicals and later erotic shows. After renovation in the 1990s, the old theaters (about 40 of them) have seen a huge wave of success with the renewed popularity of Broadway musicals.

HISTORIC THEATERS

Start with **42nd Street** where you'll find the oldest, most legendary auditoriums of the Theater District, and then head north. The **New Amsterdam Theater** (1903) hosted the New York shows of Maurice Chevalier. 44th Street also has numerous auditoriums rich in history: the **Majestic** (1927), the **Shubert Theater** (1913) where Barbra Streisand played early concerts, and the **Lambs Theater** (1904). At no. 432, in a former church, you'll find the **Actors Studio** where Marlon Brando, Dustin Hoffman and Al Pacino studied, among others. On 45th Street, the **Lyceum Theater** still retains its Beaux-Arts facade (1903). The **Imperial Theater** stages famous musicals. On 46th Street, the **Lunt-Fontanne** once welcomed Marlene Dietrich.

On 47th Street, the **Barrymore Theater** produced *A Streetcar Named Desire* with Marlon Brando. On the corner of Broadway and 50th Street, the **Cadillac Winter Garden** was the home of the Ziegfeld Follies, who performed here with Josephine Baker.

CARNEGIE HALL

C4 *156 West 57th St. (corner of 7th Ave.) - ℘ 212 247 7800 - www.carnegiehall.org - guided visit 1hr (except Jul-Aug): Mon-Fri 11.30am, 12.30pm, 2pm, 3pm; Sat 11.30am and 12.30pm - $17 (under 12s $12).*
The most famous concert hall in New York was financed by **Andrew Carnegie**, steel magnate and the son of Scottish immigrants, who was quick to become engaged with charitable works. At the end of the 19C, he decided to finance the construction of an auditorium that would be known the world over. Built in a style evocative of the Italian Renaissance, it was inaugurated on May 9, 1891, under the conducting baton of Tchaikovsky. From 1892 to 1962, this was the stage of the **New York Philharmonic Orchestra**. The interior comprises three auditoriums alternating classical, jazz and world music concerts and variety shows. The **Rose Museum** *(2nd fl. - from Oct 1-June 30: 11am-4.30pm - free)* brings together documents telling the story of more than a century of the history of Carnegie Hall.

HEARST TOWER★

C4 *300 W 57th St.*
The building of the Hearst Corporation stands out in the city's urban landscape. The base structure, designed by architect Joseph Urban

Hearst Tower designed by Foster + Partners

© L. Decoudin/Michelin

52

Stockholm Syndrome

A sensational news story in the 1970s made the name Hearst famous across the world. Patty Hearst, the granddaughter of the founder of the Hearst Company, William Randolph Hearst, was kidnapped by an extreme terrorist group, the Symbionese Liberation Army, who demanded a ransom from the family. Initially treated poorly by her jailers, she developed Stockholm Syndrome, embracing the cause of her kidnappers and participating in hold-ups, for which she was jailed.

in 1928, is made of reconstituted stone, a mix of sand and concrete. Eight allegorical statues, representing comedy, tragedy, music, art, industry, sport, science and printing, are integrated into the ribbed columns. However, the stock market crash of 1929 put an end to Art Deco construction. In 2006, a new tower created by Norman Foster would complete the original construction. The 40-story building features a modern glass facade, criss-crossed with superimposed steel triangles, which serve as supporting walls. In the lobby you'll find a sculpture called *Icefall*, made with thousands of panels of glass, forming a waterfall that uses collected rainwater. The sculpture is embellished by a 23m/75ft fresco, *Riverlines*, created by British artist Richard Long.

TIMES SQUARE ★★

C5 *Crossroads of Broadway and 7th Ave.* With its heaving sidewalks, bright lights and concert of car horns (at any hour, day or night), Times Square, in the heart of the Theater District, remains the **emblem** of the frenetic New York living.

In the 19C, **Longacre Square** served as a horse market. Its name changed in 1904 when the daily newspaper *The New York Times* decided to build offices here. In 1916, the installation of the first **electric signs** would be authorized, creating the now iconic look of this famous crossroads. In the golden age of movie production in New York, this district was the home of iconic studios, including Paramount and Twentieth Century Fox. In the 1970s, its reputation would diminish as a result of increasing drug dealing and the opening of sex shops in the neighboring streets. It became calmer once more in the 1990s.

Today, Times Square still contains many buildings of interest: at no. 1, the HQ (until 2007) of *The New York Times*; at no. 3, news agency **Reuters** and at no. 4 the high-tech former **Condé Nast** building (Condé Nast moved to 1 WTC in 2014), recognizable by its round tower covered in screens. October 2017 saw the opening of **National Geographic Encounter**, an immersive experience in the oceans of the world (though this is not an aquarium) which promises to be innovative, as it is entirely based on optical

A colossal work

The Empire State Building took only one year and 45 days to build : up to 4 000 construction workers a day worked on it, employing 60 000 tons of steel and 10 million bricks. The building has 6 500 windows, 73 ultra-fast elevators and 1 860 steps. It was meant to cost 50 million dollars, but the bill was reduced to 41 million. Its renovation, however, cost almost 100 million dollars !

illusions, and 3-D imagery and using the most up-to-date technology (natgeoencounter.com).

MADAME TUSSAUDS WAX MUSEUM

C5 234 42nd St. - ℘ 866 841 3505 - www.nycwax.com - June-Aug: 9am-10pm; rest of the year: 9/10am-8/10pm (depending on the season) - starting at $29.
This museum displays more than 200 waxworks of celebrities, and the renderings are uncannily life-like.

GARMENT DISTRICT

Stretching from 30th to 40th Sts, this was for a long time the center of **dress-making and tailoring**, once one of the main industries of New York. Today the workshops have moved down to Lower East Side, Chinatown and Brooklyn after rents here became prohibitively high.

MACY'S★

C5 151 West 34th St. (between Broadway and 7th Ave.) - www. macys.com - Mon-Sat 10am-10pm, Sun 11am-9pm.
Constructed in 1901, Macy's prides itself on being the largest store in

the world, with 10 floors of products. Every year the colorful **Thanksgiving Day Parade** is organized here (👞 p. 146).

5th AVENUE★★★

C5-D4 Like the theaters of Broadway, 5th Avenue, dotted with chic stores, is an **emblem** of New York. This impressive urban canyon splits the city in two: from Washington Square to Harlem, all streets of Manhattan are divided by this mythic avenue into **East** or **West**. Once the setting of imposing manor houses, at the beginning of the 20C, 5th Avenue became the home of department stores and luxury boutiques. It is dotted with some of the town's finest architectural treasures and, to the west until 6th Avenue, fascinating museums, including the unmissable MoMA.

EMPIRE STATE BUILDING★★★

C5 350 5th Ave. (between 33rd and 34th Sts) - ℘ 212 736 3100 - www. esbnyc.com - 8am-2am (last elevator 1.15am) - observatory on the 86th fl.: $34 (6-12 years $27, -under 6s free; Main Deck Express (skip the line) $60; optional ascent to 102bd floor $20

Empire State Building and the Manhattan skyline viewed from Top of the Rock

Koreatown

On W 32nd St. (between 5th Ave. and Broadway) and the surrounding streets, visitors can take a trip to the Land of the Morning Calm, where businesses showcase the (sometimes unknown) mainstays of Korean cuisine and entertainment. You'll find barbecue restaurants open 24hrs and karaoke bars, popular with the businessmen of Seoul, as well as CDs from K-pop stars, DVDs of Korean films, acupuncturists, etc.

on top of regular ticket; Main Deck Express (skip the line) + optional ascent to 102nd fl.: $80. Allow up to 2hrs for waiting in line.

With the collapse of the twin towers of the World Trade Center, this **legendary skyscraper** once more became the **highest in the city** (443m/ 1453ft with the antenna) until it was overtaken by One World Trade Center in 2014, which measures 541m/1775ft. The Empire State Building, built in the place of the first Waldorf-Astoria hotel, was inaugurated on May 1, 1931. The whole undertaking could have easily descended into a huge fiasco, as just after the contracts were signed, the United States was plunged into the Great Depression following the crash of 1929. However, instead, its construction would act as a galvanizing force: from its beginning, the skyscraper invited awe and fantasy. In 1933, it featured in the legendary *King Kong*, with the iconic image of the giant gorilla climbing to its summit. More tragically, in 1945, as a result of foggy conditions, a plane embedded itself in the 79th floor, killing 14. Installed in 1953, the television antenna, surpassing the original mast, was subsequently

equipped with a lantern to warn "lost" pilots. From then on, the summit of the building has been lit up every night, with colors changing depending on the occasion and season.

Observatory – Located on the 86th floor (320m/1050ft up), it offers one of the most beautiful panoramas★★★ of the city , showing the concrete forest of Midtown to the north and, beyond the lower buildings of Greenwich Village and Soho, the skyscrapers of southern Manhattan, including One World Trade Center.

NEW YORK PUBLIC LIBRARY★

C5 *5th Ave., between West 40th and 42nd Sts -* ℘ *917 275 6975 - www.nypl. org/help - Mon-Sat 10am-6pm, Sun 1pm-5pm - closed bank holidays.*
The main branch of the New York Public Library (NYPL) — one of the most significant in the world — is the work of bibliophile patrons John Jacob Astor and James Lennox, generous donor Samuel Tilden, and its executor, John Bigelow. The latter succeeded in fusing the libraries of the first two using the money of the third to construct them a unique edifice, inaugurated in 1911. Architects Carrère and Hastings were entrusted

with the design, who created one of their first Beaux-Arts style buildings. **Andrew Carnegie** would also contribute to the project. From the beautiful flight of stairs, you can admire the **colonnade** and the **pair of stone lions** that guard the entrance. If the exterior is almost intimidating in its heft, the six-level marble interior with its **spectacular glass roof** is more airy and convivial. The **collections** of books are the second largest in the country after the Library of Congress in Washington, DC.

BRYANT PARK★

C5 *Between 42nd and 40th Sts.*
Backing onto the NYPL, this park is ideal for a picnic; in summer there are concerts and films screened here. Look out for the buildings that border it. the impressive **American Standard Building** (1924), in black brick embellished with gold-coated terracotta, and the **HBO Building** housing the TV station.

DIAMOND DISTRICT

C5 *47th St , between 6th and 5th Aves.*
90 % of diamonds that enter the US pass through this street, where the largest number of **precious stones** in the world are sold each year. Started in the south of Manhattan in the 19C, this trade followed its rich clients northwards, towards 5th Avenue; approximately 2600 businesses established themselves here.

ROCKEFELLER CENTER★★★

C4 *5th Ave, between 48th and 51st Sts -*
☎ *212 588 8601 - www.rockefeller center.com.*
At inception, Rockefeller Center was a big architectural and urban concept in New York. For the first time, a vast collection of buildings was created and unified around an idea or a style. **John D. Rockefeller Jr.**, oil magnate and the richest man in the world at the time, saw in this undertaking the opportunity to develop the area. He would base the project around the nascent radio and cinema industries. Architects would create 13 buildings around a central plaza and an emblematic skyscraper rising higher than the others around it. Works of art, a garden and open spaces allowed the public to make the space their own, transmitting the image of an ideal America. Started in 1931, finished in 1939, the initial complex was, with the exception of the World Trade Center, the most ambitious project in the city's history. In 1947 and 1973, seven new buildings were constructed. It is estimated that 65000 people worked on the site.

Rockefeller Plaza★★ – You'll arrive here from 5th Avenue along the **Channel Gardens**, between the **Maison Française** and the **British Empire Building**. This narrow walkway is planted with flowers sloping down gently to Lower Plaza; there's a half-buried café encircling a large terrace, lined with flags from various countries. This is where you'll find the famous ice rink, open every winter since 1936, and the gleaming statue of **Prometheus** (Paul Manship, 1934).

General Electric Building★★ – The highest skyscraper of the complex, finished in 1933 (70 floors constructed in less than 16 months), is considered a perfect example of Art Deco, both on the outside—with its straight lines and tapering floors—and within. The entrance of the plaza is decorated with colorful bas-reliefs (Lee Lawrie, 1933), centered around the theme of "Wisdom". The lobby is even more impressive, with its huge fresco by Spanish artist José Maria Sert, entitled *American Progress* (the work replaced the "offensive" creation of Diego Rivera which depicted the May Day marches led by Lenin). On the 65th floor, don't miss the superb Art Deco restaurant Rainbow Room.

Top of the Rock★★★ – *C4* - entrance via 50th St. between 5th and 6th Aves - 67th-70th floor - ☎ 877 692 7625 - www.topoftherocknyc.com - 8am-12am (last elevator 11.15pm) - $34 (6-12 years $28), Sun & Star ticket (two visits on the same day, one in the day and one at night, ticket valid 24h) + $15 - reserve by phone or online to choose your time. Other than the Empire State Building, this is the way to get a bird's eye view of Manhattan. From the terrace (259 m/850ft), you can admire the Empire State Building and Central Park. The magnificent **atrium**★★★, spanning three glass-lined floors, presents the history of Rockefeller Center. The long, narrow observatory, reminiscent of the deck of a boat, offers a fantastic

panorama★★★ over Midtown: go at night to fully appreciate the city lights.

NBC STUDIO TOUR★

C4 30 Rockefeller Plaza - ☎ 212 664 3700 - www.nbcstudiotour.com - 8.30am-2pm on weekdays, until 5pm on the weekend (departs every 30mins) - $33 (6-12 years $29).
On this studio visit, you'll discover the history of station NBC, spanning the beginnings of radio and the transition to television.

RADIO CITY MUSIC HALL★

C4 1260 6th Ave. (corner of 50th St.). A typical example of Art Deco architecture, this music hall (1932), the largest covered theater in the world, was part of the larger complex of Rockefeller Center. Traditionally film premieres were held here. It now welcomes musical shows, of which the most popular is the *Radio City Christmas Spectacular*.

MUSEUM OF MODERN ART (MOMA)★★★

C4 11 West 53rd St. (between 5th and 6th Aves) - ☎ 212 708 9400 - www.moma.org - daily 10.30am-5.30pm (9pm Fri-Sat) - closed 25 Dec and Thanksgiving - $25 (students $14, under 16s free), free Fri 4-8pm; ticket includes entry to PS1. (👆 p. 99) - map and audio guide included w/ticket - children's audio guide available. Allow between 1hr30min to 3hrs.

Museum of Modern Art

Its light interior architecture, sculpture garden and incredible collection of masterpieces make a visit to **MoMA** a fascinating journey through the art of the 19C to the present. It was founded in 1929 by three women: **Abby Rockefeller** (whose husband created Rockefeller Center), **Lillie Bliss** and **Mary Sullivan**, who wished to create a space for modern art. Between 2002 and 2004 the museum underwent a major renovation. It was expanded and made more airy and spacious, but it retained its acquisition policy, mixing painting, sculpture, photography and design. In 2014, MoMA announced a project extending and redesigning its building. It was not without controversy, as it entailed the destruction of the emblematic building next door, which housed the Folk Art Museum. MoMA is arranged around a spectacular lobby. Take in the views out over the **Sculpture Garden★★**, which is dotted with benches and open to visitors (weather permitting).

Paintings and sculptures★★★ occupy the 4th and 5th floors *(allow 1hr30min to 2hr)*. The works do not follow a strictly chronological order and are not grouped by artist. Instead, they are grouped thematically, with the idea of showing how different artists or artistic movements can be linked, even if they are from very different eras.

The **Impressionists** are represented by Pierre Bonnard, Édouard Vuillard and Claude Monet including the triptych *Reflections of the Clouds on the Water Lily Pond* (1920), which occupies an entire room.

The **Post-Impressionists** moved towards pared-down lines and more stark colors. Among them, Georges Seurat (*Evening, Honfleur*, 1886), Paul Cézanne (*The Bather*, 1885), Paul Gauguin and Henri Rousseau. Vincent Van Gogh is celebrated with *The Olive Trees* (1889) and the famous *Starry Night* (1889).

The **Fauves**, taking in André Derain and the first works of Matisse, are identifiable by their bold rush strokes and panels of color. After this movement, Picasso developed a new painting style. His early canvasses help track his long evolution, from the soft colors and figurative models of his nudes from the Rose Period to the *Demoiselles d'Avignon* (1907), where we trace the influence of Oceanic art and the move towards **Cubism**. This is underlined in works such as *Boy leading a Horse* (1905-1906), *Woman with Pears* (1909) and *Ma Jolie* (1911-1912). It is in comparing Picasso and Georges Braque that we really begin to approach Cubism. The museum's collection contains work from Juan Gris and many pieces by Henri Matisse, brought together in a one room, including Matisse's famous *Dance.* Next, there are more Picassos, various works from Giorgio de Chirico and Fernand Léger and Brancusi sculptures.

Expressionism is characterized by depictions distorted by the emotions of the artist. Shapes are stylized and colors often bold. German artists were at the forefront of this movement, represented in the MoMA collection by paintings from Oskar Kokoschka, Paul Klee and Vassily Kandinsky (*Picture with an Archer*, 1909).

The first **abstract art** followed naturally from Cubism, but the geometric shapes and large colored surfaces were no longer used to emulate the real in any way. Among the pioneers, we find Marc Chagall, Robert Delaunay, Kazimir Malevich and Fernand Léger. In another style, the Mondrian room introduces a purely plastic form of this art.

The **Dada movement** and **surrealism** also occupy a vast room, which includes collages from Picasso and Braque. You'll find the montages of Francis Picabia, Marcel Duchamp and Kurt Schwitters. Among the great surrealists, you can admire André Breton, Joan Miró with *Hirondelle Amour* (1933), Max Ernst, René Magritte and Salvador Dalí (*The Persistence of Memory*, 1931). In terms of sculptures, there are some remarkable statues in the style of **primitive deities** from Giacometti. There is no shortage, either, of the **American painters**, with a collection spanning Edward Hopper and Charles Sheeler.

On the 4th floor, other great names of American painting are brought together with **abstract expressionism**, from the middle of the 20C to today: Helen Frankenthaler, Jackson Pollock, Willem De Kooning with *Woman I* (1950), Mark Rothko, Clyfford Still, Robert Motherwell, Robert Rauschenberg and Jasper Johns,

but also English artist Francis Bacon. Beside Andy Warhol and *Gold Marilyn Monroe* (1962), you'll find **pop art** spanning James Rosenquist, Claes Oldenburg and Roy Lichtenstein. A wing dedicated to **design★★** covers both the progress of technology in everyday objects and the development of aesthetics during the 20C, from the cooking utensils of the 1930s and 1940s to the very first computers, taking in humble and more extravagant furniture.

The **photography** department traces the history of this medium from the middle of the 19C and its journalistic, artistic and commercial applications. The collection of **drawings★** presents works in pencil, ink and charcoal, as well as collages and watercolors.

INTREPID SEA, AIR & SPACE MUSEUM★

B4 Pier 86 (at the level of 46th St.) - ✆ 212 245 0072 - www.intrepid museum.org - 10am-5pm (Sat-Sun and public holidays from April to October 6pm) - $33 ticket (13-17 years and seniors $31, 5-12 years $24).

This open-air museum brings together boats from the US Navy, including the *Intrepid* —an aircraft carrier from the Second World War, also used during the Vietnam War and the Cuban Missile Crisis**. Y**ou'll also find a collection of planes, including *Concorde,* as well as the *Enterprise*, **NASA's first space shuttle** (in the Space Shuttle Pavilion).

Midtown East ★

The eastern part of Midtown developed at the same time as its neighbor to the west, but the focus here is business rather than theatre. With the presence of Grand Central station, this area became a center for trade, and the construction of office buildings inevitably followed. The proximity to 5th Avenue attracted luxury hotels and prestigious institutions, such as The Morgan Library and the headquarters of the United Nations.

▶**Access:** 33rd St, Grand Central-42nd St, 51st St. Bus: M15, 34, M42, M50 *Detachable map CD5*.
▶**Tip:** For great photos of the Chrysler Building, use a telephoto lens and head to 3rd Avenue, between 42nd and 44th Streets. Bring binoculars to fully admire the detail of its architecture.

MURRAY HILL★

C5 Located between 30th and 40th Sts, the south part of Midtown East owes its name to Robert Murray, a merchant of English origin who would construct his "country house" here. For some time this was a quiet, leafy area occupied by bourgeois houses and the stables of the palaces of 5th Avenue. Today, the manor houses have been replaced by department stores, and the stables by residential buildings.

MORGAN LIBRARY★★

C5 *225 Madison Ave. - ☎ 212 685 0008 - www.themorgan.org - Tues-Thurs 10.30am-5pm, Fri 10.30am-9pm, Sat 10am-6pm, Sun 11am-6pm - closed Mon, 1 Jan, Thanksgiving and 25 Dec - $20 (students and 13-16 year-olds $13); free Friday from 7pm to 9pm. Allow between 1hr and 1hr30min.*

In the 19C, one of the richest men in New York, **John Pierpont Morgan** (1837-1913), built a luxurious Neoclassical-style residence in Murray Hill. In 1924, his son granted his father's wish to turn the family's private collections (of antique printed books and rare manuscripts) into a public institution. Since this time, it has been added to with donations and acquisitions. The current renovated premises bring together the homes of the father and son. The collections of **manuscripts, sheet music** and **literature** are impressive, spanning scores from Mozart, Beethoven, Brahms, Chopin, Verdi and others, without forgetting the modern Schoenberg and Cage; literary manuscripts, letters and notes from Galilei, Milton, Poe, Byron, Charles Dickens, Mark Twain, Thoreau, Oscar Wilde, John Steinbeck, Ernest Hemingway, and Jane Austen, while one of the three remaining editions of the Gutenberg Bible is painstakingly conserved in the majestic East Room. You will also find intricate bookbindings encrusted with precious gemstones and rare manuscripts, of which the oldest dates from the 7C. Sacred objects and paintings are kept in Morgan's office: Perugino's *Madonna, Portrait of a Man* by *Tintoretto, Portraits of Martin Luther and his wife* by Lucas Cranach the Elder, as well as a number of drawings by Michelangelo, da Vinci, Dürer, Rembrandt, Watteau, Goya, Ingres, Degas and Van Gogh.

GRAND CENTRAL TERMINAL★★

C5 Corner of Park Ave. South and 42ⁿᵈ St - www.grandcentralterminal. com - 5.30am-2am - folding guide available in the central kiosk- audio guide with map (seniors $9 and students $7) at counters marked GCT Tour (daily 9am-6pm); guided tour (1hr15min, $25, seniors and students $20) daily at 12.30pm organized by the Municipal Art Society of New York. In 1871, railway magnate, **Cornelius Vanderbilt** constructed a first station, which was replaced by the current edifice in 1913. On the ground site of the old station, Park Avenue and Madison Avenue were created. In the place of buildings black with soot, residences and chic hotels were built, and later skyscrapers, giving the area a fine variety of 20C architecture. With its horizontal access to the platforms, which could also be reached directly from the subway, the layout of the **station** was revolutionary at the time. In 1947,

© Graham Haber, 2014/The Morgan Library & Museum

Vault, Pierpont Morgan's Study, The Morgan Library & Museum

it was estimated that 65 million passengers swarmed through here each year; today more than 75000 pass through daily. Landmarked in 1978 and superbly renovated in 1998, it is now a hub for regional trains. Its impressive Beaux-Arts facade is adorned with a clock surrounded by Mercury, Minerva and Hercules. The **Main Concourse**, 12 stories high, is topped with a painted and electrified **vault** depicting the constellations (represented backwards; the west is found in the east!). Imposing staircases lead up to balconies. The glimmering little central kiosk is one of the mythical meeting points of the city.

63

CHRYSLER BUILDING★★★

D5 *Corner of 42nd St. and Lexington Ave.*

This is neither the tallest nor the best located skyscraper in New York, but it is incontestably the most beautiful: its finesse and refined elegance and its delicate spire are unparalleled. Built in 1930 at the behest of the car maker **Walter Chrysler**, the Chrysler Building was born of the imagination of architect **William Van Alen** who wanted to construct the tallest building in the world (319m/1046ft, 77 stories). It did not hold the record for long, as it was overtaken the following year by the Empire State Building. Its originality lies in the use of steel as an embellishment, emphasizing the play of light on its structure and accentuating its soaring silhouette. It is one of the most spectacular examples of Art Deco architecture, featuring niches, gargoyles in the shape of eagles' heads (in a nod to the Chrysler hood ornaments), alternating curved and triangular lines and a summit evoking the chrome detailing of the automobile. On the inside, the lobby is just as impressive, featuring red marble, geometrical friezes, the eagle motif and a fresco on the ceiling exploring the theme of transport and industry.

UNITED NATIONS HEADQUARTERS (UN) ★★

D5 *On the edge of the East River, between 42nd and 48th Sts, visitors' entrance 46th St. and 1st Avenue - ℰ 212 963 8687/4440 - www.un.org/fr/aboutun -guided tours only (1hr): Mon-Fri 9am-4.30pm (arrive 30min before the beginning of the tour for security checks, ID required) - closed public holidays - children under 5 not allowed - $22 (seniors and students $15, 5-12 years $13), online reservation only.*

Created on October 24, 1945, the UN is an intergovernmental community tasked with maintaining peace in the world. The decision to create the headquarters in New York was taken at the first General Assembly in 1946. The land dedicated to the project, bought thanks to a donation from John D. Rockefeller Jr., benefits from a special status placing it outside of American jurisdiction.

The visitor enters the complex via an esplanade decorated with two symbolic sculptures: *Non-Violence*, the revolver with a knotted barrel (Carl Fredrik Reuterswärd, 1988), and *Sphere Within Sphere* (Arnaldo Pomodoro, 1996). On the right, the **General Assembly Building** (1952), with its curved facade houses the United Nations General Assembly, where the delegates of member states meet. Set back on the riverside, we find the **Conference Building**, which houses conference and meeting rooms. This is the home

Chrysler Building

of, among other functions, the Security Council, composed of fifteen member states, of which only five are permanent (the US, China, Russia, France and the UK). The most famous building is the blue-gray glass skyscraper that dominates the complex: the **Secretariat Building** (1950). It houses, as its name suggests, the offices of the Secretary General and all their services.

TUDOR CITY★

D5 Created for middle-class residents by promoter Fred F. French, the idea of the complex was to create a town within a town, with 3000 apartments, a hotel, shops and green spaces. The 12 brick buildings are decorated with flower-adorned apexes in flamboyant Gothic style, evoking English Tudor style.
Odd fact: the buildings on the east side only have a few windows because, at the time of their construction, the contemporary site of the esplanade of the United Nations was an industrialized area.
From **Tudor City Place**, take the alley that crosses 42nd Street *(access via steps from 42nd and 43rd Sts)*, to discover a superb **view★.**

SAINT PATRICK'S CATHEDRAL★★

CD5 *5th Ave., between 50th and 51st Sts - www.saintpatrickscathedral.org - 6am-8pm - guided tour at 10am (see website for details).*
Enclosed between the surrounding high buildings, one of the first grand neo-Gothic churches in America seems strangely small, though its towers actually stretch to over 100m/328ft.
Inspired by Cologne Cathedral, it was conceived by architect **James Renwick Jr.** in 1879. Opposite the edifice stands the bronze statue of **Atlas** carrying the world on his shoulders (Lee Lawrie, 1937).

PALEY PARK★ AND GREENACRE PARK★

D5 *Leave 5th Ave heading east: Paley Park is on E 53rd St between 5th Ave. and Madison; Greenacre Park is on 51st St between 3rd and 2nd Aves.*
These pockets parks provide a brief escape from the hubbub of the Big Apple.
A place for meditation and relaxation, **Greenacre Park** is frequented by tourists as well as city workers savoring their lunch breaks. Take a seat on a chair dotted amid the flowers and trees, and take in the relaxing soundtrack of birdsong and the running water of an artificial waterfall, all hemmed in by walls of climbing ivy.
Closer to 5th Ave, and offering a little less charm than Greenacre Park despite a number of the same features (wall of water, tables and chairs, flowerbeds), **Paley Park** is principally known for its fragments of the Berlin Wall.

Central Park ★★★

Gone are the lines of honking taxis, the graffiti, the never-ending thrum of traffic: Central Park is a green haven, a sprawling countryside in the heart of the city. All around, the skyscrapers seem almost modest, despite their sophisticated silhouettes. Under the park's huge trees, the city is almost forgotten, and yet, New York is just there.

▶**Access:** Subway: A, B, C, and D trains run up the west side; 4, 5, and 6 run up the east side. Bus: M66, M72, M79, M86, M96 and M106 cross Central Park. *Detachable map C-D4*, *D3*, *E2*.

▶**Tip:** You can start at the southern end of the park and leave at the top (or vice versa) while visiting **Museum Mile★★★** (👁 *p. 70*) on the way. Be sure to get the full experience by stopping for a picnic. There is a supermarket at Columbus Circle and many along the avenues on the east and west side.
Central Park (www.centralparknyc.org) has 93 km/57mi of paths. Maps, event calendars and timetables available in the three welcome centers of the park (The Dairy in the center of the park, Dana Discovery Center in the north and Belvedere Castle). Tours available.

In the 18C, the north of Manhattan was the site of farms and summer residences of a few wealthy individuals. With the rise of urbanization, the bourgeois decided to live in their manor houses year-round. The central part of this zone was left as foul-smelling marshland, dotted with giant rocks, squatted on by a contingent of poor and marginalized New-Yorkers. **William Cullen Bryant** (for whom Bryant Park is named), a literary man and editor of the *New York Evening Post*, launched in 1850 a powerful press campaign with the aim of creating a park comparable to the great European green spaces.
Central Park was finished in 1873, 16 years after ground was broken. It was the work of architects and landscapers **Frederick Olmsted** and **Calvert Vaux,** who envisaged the park as a series of living tableaux presenting an ideal of nature. The project required 20000 workers, planting half a million trees and millions of feet of earth, imported by boat, which would fill the swamps and the space left by the destruction of 300000 t of rocks. In the end the Park cost the United States double the Alaska Purchase ($7.4m vs. 7.2m)! With its 341ha/842 acres, Central Park is the **green lung of New York**. Visitors come for respite from the city, but without really leaving it thanks to the surrounding crown of skyscrapers. In terms of cultural events and public celebrations, it's a major site, at the heart of all big city events. New Yorkers spontaneously gather here

in times of trouble, as happened after the September 11th attacks, or at times of dissent, against war or in favor of a humanitarian cause. After a low period that ended in the 1980s, during which parts of the park were considered unsafe, the park re-established itself as a place for families, nature-lovers, sporty types and tourists. Twenty million people come to this park every year.

WILDLIFE CENTER (CENTRAL PARK ZOO)

D4 *Apr-Oct: 10am-5pm (Sat-Sun and public holidays 5.30pm); rest of the year: 10am-4.30pm - $18 (3-12 years $13), 10 % discount online.* Above the entrance arch chimes the **Delacorte Clock** and its animated animal figurines. More than 450 animals are in this zoo, separated into three key climates (temperate, tropical and polar).

BETHESDA FOUNTAIN TERRACE★

D3-4 The Mall is a majestic alley set in the shadow of gigantic elm trees. It's overlooked in the south by a statue of Shakespeare. On its left spreads the prairie of **Sheep Meadow**, where picnickers and Frisbee throwers have replaced the sheep (the old sheep pen, to the west, has been converted into restaurant Tavern on the Green). The mall leads to **Bethesda Fountain Terrace★**, an elegant esplanade and one-time meeting point for hippies during the counter-culture movement of the 20C. Considered the master feature of the

park, this pretty sandstone terrace resembles a Spanish patio with its stairs and central statue-adorned fountain.

THE LAKE★★

D3 The Bethesda Fountain Terrace sits next to the Lake of which the irregular form is dominated by the craggy hill of the **Ramble**, criss-crossed with paths. To the west, the **Strawberry Fields** memorial garden takes its name from the song penned by John Lennon, who was assassinated at the foot of the Dakota Building, just by this point of the park. Bypassing the lake on the right, you arrive at **Loeb Boathouse**, where you can rent row boats, get something to eat or stop for a drink. You can cross the lake via the elegant metal **Bow Bridge★★**, stepping out onto the north side.

JACQUELINE KENNEDY ONASSIS RESERVOIR★

DE3 Farther to the north you'll find the Jacqueline Kennedy Onassis Reservoir, a legendary spot for joggers (Dustin Hoffman runs round it in *Marathon Man*). As you pass behind the Metropolitan Museum, note **Cleopatra's Needle**, an obelisk of which the (translated) hieroglyphics tell the story of Thutmose III (15C BC). It was given to the city of New York by the Khedive of Egypt, Isma'il Pasha (transported to the United States in 1880).

68

Central Park in autumn

Upper East Side★★★ and Museum Mile★★★

This is one of the most expensive neighborhoods in Manhattan. 5th Avenue is bursting with prestigious apartment blocks. In front of these elegant residences, you'll see door staff standing to attention, ready to welcome the moneyed residents home from their outings—a shopping trip, perhaps. All around you'll find museums housed in imposing manor houses, displaying the area's affinity to culture, as well as the generosity of wealthy patrons.

▶**Access:** Subway: lines 4, 5 and 6 between 63rd and 110th Sts and the Q at 72nd, 86th, and 96th Sts. Bus: M1 to 4, M66, M72, M79, M86, M96, M98, M101 to 103.

Detachable map DE4, DF3, E2.
▶**Tip:** The Guggenheim and Cooper Hewitt are pay what you wish Saturday evenings. The Frick is pay what you wish Wednesday 2-6pm. Expect a long line at the Guggenheim.

MUSEUM MILE★★★

This name refers to the section of 5th Avenue that runs alongside Central Park. Here, billionaires built the most splendid manor houses of the city, and then at the start of the 20C made donations to create foundations. As a result, this short section of avenue hosts a heavy concentration of some of the world's most beautiful museums, as well as the most exclusive private mansions in New York—in Beaux-Arts or Queen Anne style—adorned with opulent awnings. Starting from **Grand Army Plaza** (not to be confused with the one in Brooklyn), dominated by

the **Pulitzer Fountain** (1915) and the equestrian statue of General Sherman (1903), you can see the **General Motors Building**, the **Plaza** (1907) and The Pierre hotel, which welcomes the international jet-set. The prestigious Knickerbocker Club (1870, *no. 810*) is reserved for the descendants of the Dutch pioneers. The Beaux-Arts style **Marshall Orme Wilson House** (1903, *3 E. 64th St.*) is now the Indian consulate. **Harkness House** (1900, 1 E. *75th St.*), set in an Italian Renaissance-style mansion, is the home of the Commonwealth Fund, a philanthropic association. James B. Duke House (*1 E. 78th St.*), a Neoclassical edifice inspired by a

Louis XVI-style Bordeaux château, is the setting of the **New York Institute of Fine Arts**. The cultural and press services of the French consulate are housed in the Beaux-Arts style former residence (1906, *972 5ᵗʰ Ave.*) of Payne Whitney. The **Ukrainian Institute of America**, in a stunning little château in French Renaissance style (1897, *2 E. 79ᵗʰ St.*), is housed in the residence of the Sluyvesants, descendants of the first governor of New York. The former **Goethe House** (1957, *1014 5th Avenue between 82ⁿᵈ and 83ʳᵈ Sts*) is a Beaux-Arts style residence.

TEMPLE EMANU-EL★

D4 *1 East 65ᵗʰ St. - 𝒫 212 744 1400 - www.emanuelnyc.org - daily except Fri and Sat 10am-4.30pm (call before visiting) - no visiting on Jewish holidays.* With a capacity of 2500 worshippers, this Roman Moorish-Byzantine style synagogue (1929) is one of the largest in the world. Its majestic nave is covered in oriental motif mosaics. A sacred arch encloses the scrolls of the Torah. A small **museum** houses a collection of liturgical objects and hosts temporary exhibitions.

THE FRICK COLLECTION★★★

D4 *1 East 70ᵗʰ St. - 𝒫 212 288 0700 - www.frick.org - daily except Mon 10am-6pm, Sun 11am-5pm - closed public holidays - $22 (students $12); free Wed 2-6pm - audio guide included in the ticket - an introductory film (11min) is projected every 20min in the music room- under 10s not permitted, 10-16 -year-olds must be accompanied by an adult. Allow 2-3hrs.*

This delectable little museum is an ideal initiation to classical painting. Millionaire steel magnate **Henry Frick** (1849-1919) asked architects Carrère and Hastings to build him a prestigious manor house in Neoclassical style close to Central Park (1913). An art enthusiast, he would exhibit part of his magnificent collection here, which he acquired in Europe. On his death, he bequeathed his residence and the artwork to an administrative council, who would turn them into a museum in 1935. The **Boucher Room** and the **Anteroom** recreate an 18C boudoir, decorated with tableaux by François Boucher (1752). The furnishings comprise a Riesener mahogany flat desk (18C), Sèvres porcelain pieces and an Indian rug (16C). In the antechamber hangs the oldest portrait by Hans Memling. The **Dining Room** is decorated with English paintings by Hogarth, Romney, Reynolds Gainsborough and James Park. The **West Vestibule** presents *The Four Seasons* by Boucher (1775) as well as a bureau by Charles Boulle. Eleven canvases by Fragonard *(The Progress of Love)* are conserved in the **Fragonard Room**, accompanied by magnificent furnishings from the School of Paris, Sèvres porcelain and a marble bust of the Countess of Cayla, by Houdon. The **South Hall** exhibits three of Vermeer's 37 known canvases : *Officer and Laughing Girl* (around 1658), *Girl Interrupted at Her Music* (around 1660) and

Mistress and Maid (around 1666). The **Living Hall** is filled with major works: *Saint Francis* by Bellini, *Portrait of a Man in a Red Cap* by Titian, two portraits by Holbein the Younger and *Saint Jerome* by El Greco. Some fine smaller paintings from the English school are presented in the **Library**. In the **North Hall** you'll find the famous portrait *The Countess of Haussonville* by Ingres, *The Portal of Valenciennes* by Watteau, a Degas, a Monet and a Houdon bust. The largest room in the museum, the **West Gallery**, decorated with Italian furniture from the 16C, is adorned with works from the Italian, Dutch, Spanish, English and French schools: Bronzino, Véronèse, Van Dyck, Hobbema, Van Ruysdael, Frans Hals, de La Tour, El Greco, Rembrandt, Goya, Vélasquez and Turner. Visitors can admire a collection of painted enamels from the Limoges school of the 16 and 17C, as well as Italian primitives and Renaissance in the **Enamel Room**. The **Oval Room** is the setting of a rare terracotta replica of *Diana the Huntress* by Houdon. The **East Gallery** brings together exquisite works from Claude Lorrain, Greuze, Goya, Gainsborough, Van Dyck and Van Ruysdael. In the **Garden Court**, you can admire Manet's *The Bullfight* and a Whistler seascape.

MET BREUER★★

D4 Ⓜ 6 (station 77th Street). Bus M1-4, M101-M103. 945 Madison Ave. (corner of E 75th St.) - ℘ 212 731 1675 - www.metmuseum.org/visit/met-breuer - Tue-Thur 10am-5.30pm, Fri-Sat 10am-9pm,

Sun 10am-5.30pm - closed Mon - $25 (seniors $17, students $12), ticket valid for 3 consecutive days at The Cloisters (◔ p. 94) and The Met Breuer (◔ p. 72).

When the Whitney Museum moved to Meatpacking (◔ p. 45), the Met set up home in its concrete and granite building, created in 1966 by Hungarian architect Marcel Breuer. Thanks to the billionaire Leonard Lauder, son of cosmetics giant Estée Lauder, the Met was able to enrich its offer of contemporary and modern art (which was really lacking up to this point) and today competes with the Whitney, the Museum of Modern Art (MoMA) and the Guggenheim, which themselves have significant collections.

Playing with time periods, the Met Breuer presents **themed exhibitions** where the classic masters (Rembrandt, Turner and Cézanne) are blended with essential figures of modern and contemporary art (Jackson Pollock, Picasso and Robert Rauschenberg).

ASIA SOCIETY AND MUSEUM★★

D4 725 Park Ave. (corner of 70th St.) - ℘ 212 288 6400 - asiasociety.org/arts/asia-society-museum - daily except Mon 11am-6pm (Fri 9pm Sep-June) - closed public holidays - $12 (under 16s free); free Friday (except Jul-Aug) - audio guide included. Founded by **John D. Rockefeller III** (1956), this space is both a museum and a cultural center exploring art and design, but also the relationship between West and East. The superbly

Fragonard Room, The Frick Collection

curated **collections**★★ span the whole Indian subcontinent, the Himalayas, Southeast Asia, China, Korea and Japan. The building's **architecture**★ is remarkable with its steel and blue glass **staircase** linking the levels.

METROPOLITAN MUSEUM OF ART (MET)★★★

D3 5th Ave. (facing East 82nd St.) - Ⓜ lines 4, 5 and 6 (station 86th Street). Bus lines 1, 2, 3 and 4 (station 82nd Street) - ℘ 212 535 7710 - www.metmuseum.org - Sun-Thur 10am-5.30pm, Fri-Sat 10am-9pm - closed Jan 1, Thanksgiving and Dec 25 - $25 (seniors $17, students $12), ticket valid for 3 consecutive days at The Cloisters (Ⓖ p. 94) and The Met Breuer (Ⓖ p. 72); audio guide of the highlights $7 - guided tour included in the price of the ticket - map of museum at the information kiosk at the entrance. Allow 1-3hrs.

This legendary museum, one of the four or five leaders of its kind in the world, stretches in grand style off 5th Avenue, framed by heavy columns and surrounded by Central Park. Its carefully curated collections span Sumerian antiquities to the art of the 20C. The museum, which owes its existence to a number of bequests and donations from rich patrons, was created in 1870. Its Beaux-Arts facade dates from 1902, but the north and south wings are from 1911 and 1913 respectively. Other structural additions followed, such as the Lehman Pavilion (1975), the Sackler Wing (1978), the Petrie Court (1990), the Greek and Roman rooms (2007) and the section dedicated to Oceanic art.

Greek and Roman antiquities★★

First floor (ground floor), rooms 150-172, and second floor (first floor), rooms 173-176. These rooms present the roots of Western art, from Greek prehistory to the end of the Roman Empire. The history of Greek art is traced from the **Geometric Period** (8C BCE) to the **Hellenistic period** (3rd-2ndC BCE), taking in the **Archaic** and **Classical** period. Roman civilization is also well represented with the sophisticated reconstruction of a bedroom from the era, adorned with superb frescoes (1C BCE.). Don't miss the vestiges of the **Etruscan civilization**. On the first floor, there is a gallery dedicated to **Cypriot art** with the stunning *Amathus sarcophagus* (5C BCE).

Art of Africa, the Americas and Oceania ★★★

First floor (ground floor), rooms 350-359. **Nelson Rockefeller** made a donation of part of his collection in memory of his son Michael, who disappeared in 1961 on an expedition in New Guinea.

Art of Africa – More or less every facet of the ritual art of the major African tribes are presented here. Masks and statues constitute the biggest part of the collection, with some rarities, such as a sitting statuette, *Seated Figure* (Mali, 13C), a poignant evocation of the desolation of grief. The Dogon masks are particularly beautiful, as are the Benin bronzes.

74

Melanesia Gallery, Art of Africa, the Americas and Oceania, Metropolitan Museum of Art

Art of the Americas – The furniture exhibited evokes diverse civilizations from Mexico, Peru, Colombia and Ecuador. Don't miss the **Jan Mitchell Treasury**, an incredible series of pre-Columbian gold (from 1-16C.). The sumptuous ceremonial knives in gold and turquoise, the death masks, such as the mask of Sícán (Peru, 1011C), the beaten gold cups, the figurines and jewelry are all fascinating.

Arts of Oceania – The more pared down Oceanic statuettes undoubtedly inspired the silhouettes painted by Matisse and Picasso. Note the fly whisks in ivory and whale bone of Tahitian king Pomare II (18C). Among the masks, those from the Solomon Islands and Vanuatu are particularly spectacular. The collection of ritual objects from Papua New Guinea exhibits a striking sobriety.

Modern art★★★

First *(rooms 900-926) and* second *(rooms 917-925)* floors, *mezzanine.* American painting of the 20C is represented by linchpins Edward Hopper, Georgia O'Keeffe, Stuart Davis, Charles Sheeler, Arthur Dove and Marsden Hartley. The international modern art collection centers around major figures such as Picasso (*Seated Harlequin*, 1901), *The Actor* (1904-1905), *Cavalier and Seated Nude* (1967). Admire Matisse and his *Young Sailor* (1906), Balthus and *The Mountain* (1937) and the paintings and statuettes of Giacometti. You can discover the first works of Joan Miró, Dubuffet and his *View of Paris with Furtive*

Pedestrians (1944), as well as Yves Tanguy, Max Ernst and Dalí. Don't miss the delightful Bonnards (*Après la toilette du matin*, 1910) and the colorful canvases of Derain (*The Sunken Path, L'Estaque*, 1906). Among the other famous pieces, stop to contemplate *Jeanne Hébuterne* (1919) by Modigliani, the Paul Klees, including *Redgreen and Violet-Yellow Rhythms* (1920). Next you will come to the most famous Americans of the 20C: Louise Bourgeois, Clyfford Still, Rothko, Franz Kline, Willem De Kooning (*Woman*, 1944), Jackson Pollock and the stars of pop art, Andy Warhol and Roy Lichtenstein. The roof terrace hosts monumental sculpture exhibitions.

Decorative arts and European sculpture★★

First floor *(ground floor), rooms 500-556.* The period covered by the **sculptures** goes from the Renaissance to the start of the 20C. Highlights include Houdon, Rodin and several Italian sculptors. The **decorative arts** collection takes in furniture, ceramics, textiles, painting, fine gold and silver work and glassware. Reconstructions of rooms give an idea of the successive style trends of England and France in particular.

Medieval art★★★

First floor *(ground floor), rooms 300-307.* This enormous collection, organized around a central hall, brings together more than 4 000 works of art, from the fall of the Roman Empire to the Renaissance. It spans the major waves of medieval art, from Byzantium and its influence on the

76

Metropolitan Museum of Art, 5th Avenue

Flemish, English, Italian and French styles.

Among the remarkable pieces, it is worth drawing attention to the stunning rosary beads★★ in ivory or wood sculpted from delicate religious scenes, the **cut-away enamel cases**★★★ (Limoges, 12C-13C),the exceptional altarpiece★★★ in bone and ivory recounting the lives of Jesus, John the Baptist and John the Evangelist (Northern Italy, 1390-1400), as well as the painted altarpieces of the 15C and 16C. Among the collections of sacred treasures, you'll also find spectacular objects such as a series of reliquaries★★ as well as processional crosses and objects of worship.

The Robert Lehman Collection★★

First floor *(ground floor)*, rooms 950-965. The collections of this banker and his son—taking in furniture, painting and sculpture—are displayed in rooms resembling those of the home of the donors. Here you'll find Italian Primitives, including a superb *Nativity* (1409) by Lorenzo Monaco and an *Annunciation* (1485) by Botticelli; Dutch painters, with an *Annunciation* by Hans Memling; and some French impressionists, including the *Two Young Girls at the Piano* (1892) by Renoir. Note also the *Nude in Front of a Mantel* (1955) by Balthus.

American Wing★★★

First *(rooms 700-774) and* second *(703-772) floors, mezzanine.* Only American painters born before 1876 (with the exception of The Eight) are exhibited here, with the others housed with modern art (♿ p. 74).

American decorative arts – A series of reconstructions of furnished rooms chart the evolution of styles and European influences throughout the 19C. (William and Mary style, Queen Anne style, Chippendale style, the Arts and Crafts movement).

The typically American **Prairie School** is illustrated by the famous Francis W. Little House (Wayzata, Minnesota, 1912-1914), of which we can see the living room, decorated by Frank Lloyd Wright. Make a stop at **The Charles Engelhard Court** to admire the windows by Tiffany, glass-maker close to the Art Nouveau movement.

Painting and sculpture – Painting during the **Colonial period** largely featured portraits and heroic scenes. From the **Hudson School**, three works stand out: the *View from Mount Holyoke, Northampton, Massachusetts, after a Thunderstorm* (1835) by Thomas Cole; *Fur Traders Descending the Missouri* (1845) by George C. Bingham; and *View of Rocky Mountains* (1863) by Albert Bierstadt. The works of the **Post-Impressionists** James McNeill Whistler (1834-1903), John Singer-Sargent (1856-1925) and Mary Cassatt (1844-1926) are at the forefront.

Sculpture is represented by, among others, *The Mountain Man* by Frederic Remington.

Egyptian antiquities★★

First floor *(ground floor), rooms 100-138.* This collection, considered one of the richest in the world outside of Egypt, covers all aspects of Egyptian civilization. The objects are presented chronologically, from the predynastic period (starting from 5000 BCE) until the end of the Egyptian dynasties and the era of classical antiquity (700 AD). Among the treasures on display, note the **chapel of the Tomb of Perneb**★ (2450 BCE), the Chair of Reniseneb★★ (1450 BC), a rare series of **statues of the queen Hatshepsut** (around 1500-1450 BCE) and ceremonial coffins including the **Sarcophagus of Harkhebit**★. The **Temple of Dendur**★ (around 15 BCE), dedicated to the goddess Isis, was saved during the laying of the Aswan Dam and given to the US in 1965. Finally, don't miss the famous **portraits of Fayum**★★ from the Roman era.

Ancient Near Eastern Art

Second floor *(first floor), rooms 400-406).* This section covers a vast geographical zone, from Turkey to Afghanistan, taking in the Caucasus Mountains to the north of the Arabian Peninsula. The antiquities date from 8000BCE to 651 AD. The diversity of cultures that emerged in this space created great artistic richness.

The **Sackler Gallery** recreates an audience hall in the palace of Ashurnasirpal II at Nimrud.

Islamic art★★
Second floor *(first floor), rooms 450-464*. It starts at the beginning of the founding of Islam in the 7C, and continues to the 19C. Beautiful calligraphies sit side-by-side with marvelous miniatures, ceramics, mosaics, jewelry, and sumptuous textiles and rugs.

19C century painting and sculpture★★★
Second floor *(first floor), rooms 800-830*. No museum in the world has such a high concentration of major artists and world-famous works. **Impressionism** is one of the best represented currents here with Renoir, Monet, Manet, Corot and Degas. Among their works, don't miss Renoir's *Bouquet of Chrysanthemums* (1881) and *In the Meadow* (1888-1892). From Monet, you'll find *Poppy Fields near Argenteuil* (1875), *Haystacks* (1891), *Rouen Cathedral: The Portal* (1894), *Water Lilies* (1891). From Manet, *Boating* (1874) and *The Monet Family in Their Garden at Argenteuil* (1874). The works of **Degas**, spread over several rooms, depict his favorite subjects: female bathers and dancers and horses.

Among the **Post-Impressionists**, be sure to see, from Van Gogh, *Cypresses* (1890) and *La Berceuse* (1888-1889); from Seurat, the subtle *Parade (Circus Sideshow*, 1888); from Cézanne, *Bathers* (1874-1875), *The Card Players* (1890), and from Courbet, *Woman with a Parrot* (1866).

European painting★★★
Second floor *(first floor), rooms 600-644*. All the European schools of painting, from the Middle Ages to the 18C, are admirably represented. Among the masterpieces of the **Italian schools** (Florence, Venice, Sienna), look for *The Epiphany* (1320) by Giotto, *Portrait of a Woman with a Man at a Casement* (1440) by Filippo Lippi and The Last Communion of Saint Jerome (1490) by Botticelli. You should also see *The Musicians* (1595) by Caravaggio and the canvasses by Raphael, Titian and Tiepolo. The **Spanish school** is represented by striking paintings, such as the *The View of Toledo* (1595) by El Greco, or the portrait of *Manuel Osorio Manrique de Zuñiga* (1790) by Goya. Of the **northern schools** of Flanders, Holland and Germany, be sure to see the portraits by Hans Memling, *The Last Judgement* (1425); *The Harvesters* (1565) by Bruegel; *Young Man and Woman in an Inn* (1623) by Frans Hals; *Aristotle with a Bust of Homer* (1653) by Rembrandt and the marvelous *Young Woman with a Water Pitcher* (1662) by Vermeer. The **French school** brings together *The Fortune Teller* (1630) by Georges de La Tour, *The Abduction of the Sabine Women* (1633-1634) by Poussin and Mezzetin (1718-1720) by Watteau.

Asian art★★★
Second and third floors (1st and 2nd floors), rooms 200-253.

Chinese art – As well as a reconstruction of a Ming dynasty-era court, the museum presents

79

a fine variety of Chinese funerary art, ceramics, bronze objects and **paintings★★**, covering a vast period from the neolithic era (3rd millennium BCE) to the present day. A part of the exhibit is dedicated to Tibet, with superb painted panels and a Buddha dating from the 11C.

Korean art– The lesser known Korean work features impressive vases and **ceramic and bronze utensils★★**, as well as prehistoric pottery, and particularly beautiful lacquered and encrusted cases★.

Japanese art – You will see a series of **screens★**, painted panels, **prints★★** from the 18C and 19C, elegant cases and a collection of *netsukes★*, charms which served as counterweights used for attaching small hip flasks and other items to belts.

Southeast Asia – From Nepal to India, taking in Thailand, Cambodia and Indonesia, these rooms present the pantheon of Hindu divinities and impressive Khmer sculptures.

NEUE GALERIE★

E3 1048 5*th* Ave. (between 82*nd* and 83*rd* Sts) - ℘ 212 628 6200 - www. neuegalerie.org - daily except Tue and Wed 11am-6pm, guided tour (1hr) Fri-Mon at 3.30pm - $20 (seniors $15 and students $10); free 1st Fri of the month 6-9pm - audio guide available to download on website - under 12s not admitted, 12-16 year-olds accompanied by an adult. Allow 1hr.* This Beaux-Arts mansion, once the home of the Vanderbilts, has since 2001 housed the Austrian and

German art collections of cosmetics heir and businessman **Ronald Lauder** and of the art dealer **Serge Sabarsky**. The collection spans works by Egon Schiele, Gustav Klimt (including the precious *Portrait of Adele Bloch-Bauer I*, 1907), Oskar Kokoschka, Kandinsky, Paul Klee and George Grosz. Look for furnishings and pieces of decorative art from the Wiener Werkstätte school.

SOLOMON R. GUGGENHEIM MUSEUM★★

E3 1071 5*th* Ave. - ℘ 212 423 3500 - www.guggenheim.org -daily except Thur 10am-5.45pm (Sat 7.45pm) - closed 25 Dec - $25 (students and seniors $18); pay what you wish Sat. 5.45pm-7.45pm - guided tour at 2pm.* The Guggenheim Foundation, created in 1937 by **Solomon R. Guggenheim**, is a conservatory of contemporary art and an icon of modern architecture. The edifice (1956) conceived by **Frank Lloyd Wright**, likened by some to a washing machine, takes the form of a splayed out spiral. On entering, the visitor is immediately struck by the famous helical ramp (400m/1312ft) and the glass roof. The **Kandinsky Gallery★★★** exhibits a selection of the some 200 works by the artist in the museum's permanent collection, one of the largest in the world. The **Thannhauser Collection** features 75 Impressionist and Post-Impressionist works. Among the collection, you'll find *Woman Ironing* by Picasso and *In the Vanilla Grove, Man and Horse* by Gauguin.

The rest of the museum presents a rolling collection of 20C artists, including Brancusi, Calder, Marc Chagall, Paul Klee, Robert Delaunay and Joan Miró. The museum collection is also enriched by Dada pieces and surrealist works, donated by Peggy Guggenheim; all in all, there are 6000 works in the collection.

COOPER-HEWITT DESIGN MUSEUM★★

E3 2 East 91st St. (corner of 5th Ave.) - 𝒫 212 849 8400 - www.cooperhewitt. org - Mon-Fri & Sun. 10am-6pm, Sat 10am-9pm (pay what you wish from 6pm Sat.) $16 (students 19+ $7, seniors $10; buy online). Allow 1hr to 1hr30min.
This imposing 63-room mansion (1902) belonged to steel millionaire **Andrew Carnegie**. The museum, originally founded in 1897 in the building of the Cooper Union, moved here in 1976. It's the only American museum exclusively dedicated to **decorative arts**, with an emphasis on **design** spanning cultures, eras and continents. After three years of construction, the museum reopened in 2015 with an expanded exhibition space and a **new, innovative concept** : at the entrance, an interactive pen is lent to visitors who becomes veritable designers, with the ability to interact across fifteen screens spread around the museum, navigating through the objects of the collection, including those that are not exhibited in the galleries. Back home the visitor can retrace their steps on the museum's website. Don't forget to explore the gardens, which give an idea of how the Belle Époque New York gentry lived.

JEWISH MUSEUM★

E3 1109 5th Ave. (corner of 92nd St.) - 𝒫 212 423 3200 - www.thejewish museum.org - daily except Wed 11am-5.45pm (Thur 8pm) - closed public holidays and Jewish holidays $15 (under 18s free); free all Sat and Thurs 5-8pm. Allow 30-60min. Founded in 1904 in a beautiful French Neo-Gothic edifice owned by banker **Felix Warburg**, this museum tells the story of 4000 years of Jewish history through some 28000 objects, including a Torah ark dating from the 12C, exquisite bindings, ancient textiles and ritual vases.

MUSEUM OF THE CITY OF NEW YORK★★

E2 Corner 5th Ave. and 103rd St. - 𝒫 212 534 1672 - www.mcny.org - 10am-6pm - closed Jan 1, Thanksgiving and Dec 25 - suggested contribution $18 (seniors and students $12, -under 18s free). This Neo-Georgian mansion traces the history of the city via **reconstructions of interiors★★** (17-19C), including two rooms inspired by Rockefeller's house, a collection of functional and decorative objects, as well as scale models. Maritime history and the history of the port are evoked. A collection of teddy bears and exquisite **dolls' houses★★** will delight children and grown-ups alike.

81

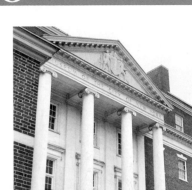

Museum of the City of New York & Museum

82

EL MUSEO DEL BARRIO★

E2 *1230 5th Ave. (near 104th St) -* ℘ *212 831 7272 - www.elmuseo.org - Wed-Sat 11am-6pm, Sun 12-5pm - suggested contribution $9 (students $5; under 12s free); Free Wed for seniors.* This museum, created in 1969 on the edge of Harlem's Hispanic district, **El Barrio**, is dedicated to Latino-American and Caribbean cultures. It encourages the creativity of this community by displaying the work of young artists in temporary exhibitions. Its pre-Columbian and contemporary collections are rarely presented to the public.

GRACIE MANSION★

F3 *East End Ave. at 89th St.) - www. nyc.gov - guided tour (45min) Tues at 10am, 11am, 2pm and 3pm - advance booking essential (for max. 2 people) on the website - $7 - arrive 5min before with your ID.*
This ravishing manor (1799), the official residence of the mayor of New York, is a perfect example of the Federal style, with its covered galleries and green shutters.

ROOSEVELT ISLAND TRAMWAY★

D4 *2nd Ave. (between 59th and 60th Sts) - http://rioc.ny.gov/ tramtransportation.htm every 15min (7-8min during rush hour 7am-10am and 3pm-8pm Mon-Fri), Sun-Thur 6am-2am, Fri-Sat 6am-3.30am - use Metrocard.*
Parallel to Queensboro Bridge, this cable car offers a surprising view of the city. The journey only lasts a few minutes, but the capsule rises rapidly above the water's edge, providing a fine view of Manhattan (especially at night). On the other side, Roosevelt Island is far quieter than Midtown just across the river.

© tupungato/iStockphoto.com

Roosevelt Island Tramway and Queensboro Bridge

Upper West Side★★ *and Morningside Heights*★★

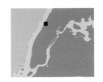

Less chic than the Upper East Side, this area nonetheless remains a bastion of the intellectual elite. With Lincoln Center and its prestigious concerts and Columbia University, this is the home of many well-off liberals and is more laid-back than its rival to the east of Central Park. Here, you'll find the upper crust of the literary and artistic worlds, having lofty conversations to a soundtrack of jazz, opera and world music. The avenues are lined with bookshops and cafés with outdoor seating.

▶**Access:** Subway: Stations between Columbus Circle and Cathedral Parkway, on lines 1, 2, 3 and A, B, C, D. Bus: M7, M10, M11, M79, M86, M96, M116.
Detachable map C2-3-4, D1-2-3.
▶**Tip:** Start at Columbus Circle, continue on foot to the Museum of Natural History, then take the bus up to Columbia. Book in advance if you want to go to a concert at Lincoln Center.

UPPER WEST SIDE★★

Unlike the rest of the city, the Upper West Side was built from the north, on the site of Nieuw Haarlem, founded in the 17C, at the level of today's 125th St. , toward the south. It was the arrival of the raised rail track that sealed its development. The creation of Columbia University (1897) made this a magnet for the intellectual elite, writers, musicians and the Jewish bourgeoisie

COLUMBUS CIRCLE

C4 On the southwest corner of Central Park, the crossroads of Columbus Circle, dominated by the statue of Christopher Columbus (1894), marks the start of the Upper West Side. At the entrance of the park, the **Maine Monument** (1913) pays homage to the 260 sailors of the battleship *Maine* destroyed in the port of Havana in 1898. The glass-walled bar of the Mandarin Oriental hotel offers a magnificent view over the city.

MUSEUM OF ARTS AND DESIGN★

C4 *2 Columbus Circle (facing Central Park) - ✆ 212 299 7777 - www. madmuseum.org - 10am-6pm (Thur 9pm), guided tours of 1hr at 11.30am and 3pm - closed Mon and*

public holidays - $16 (seniors $14 and students $12, under 18s free, pay what you wish Thur. from 6pm).

The MAD presents a collection of superb objects displaying elegant design, sublime sobriety or complicated embellishments. You'll find glass, ceramics, interior decorations, works of contemporary art, but also jewelry and painting, as well as objects taking unusual forms and using unusual materials (plastics, gypsum and even ash). On the 6th floor, three artists' studios are open to the public; on the 9th is chic restaurant Robert, known for its great view over Central Park.

TIME WARNER CENTER

C4 The southwest of Columbus Circle is occupied by this imposing building (2004) with a concave facade. The base houses a shopping center and grocery store, and the building then splits into two 80-story glass towers, of which a section is occupied by the Time Warner offices.

LINCOLN CENTER★

C4 Broadway, between 62nd and 66th Sts - ℘ 212 875 5456 - www.lincolncenter.org.

This enormous cultural complex houses 12 of the most prestigious artistic institutions in New York, including five auditoriums, a library and a school. The idea to gather all these artistic venues in one place came in 1955. The construction of Lincoln Center necessitated the razing of 188 buildings in this formerly insalubrious area, the neighborhood in which *West Side Story* was set. John D. Rockefeller III was the president of the construction committee. The central plaza sits in front of the **Metropolitan Opera House**, which hosts productions from the Metropolitan Opera and the American Ballet Theatre. On the right, the **Avery Fischer Hall** houses the New York Philharmonic, formerly based in Carnegie Hall. In the **New York State Theater** opposite that you'll find the New York City Opera and the City Ballet. On the other side of 65th Street, you'll find the famous Juilliard School.

AMERICAN FOLK ART MUSEUM★★

85

C4 2 Lincoln Square, Columbus Ave. (between 65th and 66th Sts) - ℘ 212 595 9533 - www.folkartmuseum.org - Tue-Thur 11.30am-7pm, Fri 12pm-7.30pm, Sat 11.30am-7pm, Sun 12pm-6pm - closed Mon and public holidays - free.

This museum was housed in a modern building next to the MoMA for 10 years before returning to its first historic home in July 2011, where the collection is displayed in rotation. Functional objects from the colonial age and the different eras of immigration are displayed with furniture, fabrics, spectacular weathervanes, naïve paintings and works of outsider art.

DAKOTA BUILDING

D3 *1 West 72nd St.* It is in front of the entrance of The Dakota apartments that **John Lennon** was assassinated in 1980. Previously, this beautiful Neo-Gothic building served as the backdrop for the film *Rosemary's Baby*, directed by Roman Polanski. Lauren Bacall and Judy Garland also lived here.

NEW YORK HISTORICAL SOCIETY★★

D3 *170 Central Park West (corner of 77th St.) - ℘ 212 873 3400 - www. nyhistory.org - Tue-Sat 10am-6pm (Fri 8pm), Sun 11am-5pm - closed Mon - guided tours at 2pm, 3.30pm - $21 (5-13 years $6); free entry Friday from 6pm-8pm. Allow 1hr.*
Founded in 1804 to preserve the history of the city, this institution brings together a library and a museum conserving various *objets d'art*, a fine series of paintings from the **Hudson School** and more than 400 watercolors by**John J. Audubon**, including a preparatory series for the *Birds of America*. The temporary exhibitions draw from the collections, selecting pieces according to themes related to the city. The **Henry Luce Center for the Study of American Culture** (2000) is organized like a storehouse for the museum, with huge glass cabinets, filled with almost 40 000 objects of all kinds: games, utensils, Tiffany lamps as well as George Washington's camp bed. On the basement level you'll find a fun and educational circuit, aimed at children.

AMERICAN MUSEUM OF NATURAL HISTORY★★★

D3 *Central Park West (entre 77th and 81st Sts) - ℘ 212 769 5100 - www. amnh.org - 10am-5.45pm - closed Thanksgiving and 25 Dec - pay what you wish - suggested admission $22 (2-12 years $12.50), combined ticket with the Rose Center; there are a number of ticket prices, depending on whether visitors include Hayden Planetarium (Space Show), IMAX and the temporary exhibitions - audio guide - free tour s leave from lobby on the hour, every quarter of an hour.*
The immense, magnificent **Museum of Natural History**, along with its scientific library, is one of the largest in the world. Its research center specializing in biology, anthropology and astrophysics also has an excellent reputation. Started in 1874, the monument with its hodgepodge of styles was only finished in the 1930s. Its most spectacular extension is the **Rose Center for Earth and Space★★**, an impressive glass cube (2000). But it was the museum's anthropologists in particular that gave the institution its standing, carrying out many expeditions and studies at the end of the 19C and start of the 20C. The **Theodore Roosevelt Memorial Hall★★** presents a 16.8m/55ft reconstitution of a Barosaurus skeleton. The **Hall of Biodiversity** (*ground floor*) evokes contemporary biological issues. Next is the **Hall of Ocean Life**, and then a series of rooms exploring the **environment of North America** and one more specifically dedicated to the environment of New York State. In

Fountains at Columbus Circle

©AMNH/D. Finnin

Barosaurus skeleton in the Theodore Roosevelt Rotunda, American Museum of Natural History

88

The first floor is divided into four themes: **the peoples of Africa**, the **peoples of Asia**, the **peoples of Latin America**, and a section dedicated to **birds**. Dioramas place animals and people in the context of the given continent. More than 60 000 objects reproduce the daily life of dozens of tribes. The **birds** of the Southern Seas and from across the world are stuffed to stunning effect.

The second floor brings together rooms dedicated to ethnology, in particular the **American Indians (Native Americans) of the Eastern Woodland and the Plains**, including reconstructions of their cabins. A little further along, the superb **Hall of Pacific Peoples**, filled with beautiful pieces (and dedicated to Margaret Mead) is at once bright and intimate, making it a good place to stop for contemplation. In the animal world, you'll find reptiles, primates and birds from North America.

The third floor houses six superb **Fossil Halls**. Here you may discover the first vertebra of the dinosaurs (including a *Tyrannosaurus rex*), as well as mammals and their ancestors (mammoths, giant ground sloths).

Rose Center for Earth and Space★★ – *Space Show from 10.30am-4.30pm every 30min - free audio guide.*
The scientific representation of the cosmos employs cutting edge audiovisual techniques. The **Space Theater** (in the Hayden Planetarium) is worth visiting just for its **Star Show**, a 3D presentation of a journey through space, refined with the help of NASA. At the foot of the sphere, **Scales of the Universe**

the **Northwest Coast Hall**, exploring the indigenous cultures of this region, admire the vast cedar canoe, collections of Amerindian and Inuit craft, as well as totem poles. Coming back towards the entrance hall, finish the visit with the mammals of North America.

The back of this floor, past the **Hall of Human Biology and Evolution**, is specifically dedicated to geology, with a **Hall of Meteorites** (a major piece is the 34 t fragment of meteorite found in Greenland in 1895) and a room **dedicated to minerals and precious stones** (some 4 000 specimens including the *Star of India*, a 563-carat sapphire, the largest in the world).

is a 120m/394ft-long exhibition illustrating the history of our universe. A short presentation succinctly explains the Big Bang. The **Hall of Planet Earth** presents more specifically the history of our planet and its geological and climactic evolution. Finally, the **Hall of the Universe** retransmits images from the Hubble Telescope.

CATHEDRAL OF SAINT JOHN THE DIVINE★★

D2 1047 Amsterdam Ave. (opposite 112nd St.) - www.stjohndivine.org - 7.30am-6pm.
Constructed for the Episcopal Church (1892), it can welcome up to 3000 worshippers. Today it's also a cultural space, and hosts music and art shows. The west facade, flanked by two unfinished towers, is centered around the **Portal of Paradise**; its bronze doors were made by the Parisian founder who worked on the Statue of Liberty. The immense nave is punctuated with 14 bays. Behind the choir, the radiating chapels are dedicated to seven different immigrant populations in the United States. The central chapel contains a silver triptych by pop artist Keith Haring (1989).

COLUMBIA UNIVERSITY★★

D1 From 114th to 120th St. - main entrance on Broadway at 116th St. - www.columbia.edu - Visitor Center (𝒢 212 854 4900) in Low Memorial Library: daily except Sat-Sun 9am-5pm - download app for self-guided visit.

Visitors can walk freely around campus and in the Low Memorial Library (access to other buildings permitted only with guide).
Founded in 1754 by the English under the name King's College, it was renamed Columbia College after the American Revolution. It is a private university, and one of the most prestigious in the country and a member of the Ivy League, the group of eight very selective universities on the East Coast. It is known for its scientific departments (anthropology, genetics, biotechnology), law and business. Since 1902, it has housed a school of journalism founded by publisher Joseph Pulitzer. It is this institution that awards each year the prestigious prize of the same name. Among its famous students are 37 Nobel Prize winners, presidents Roosevelt and Eisenhower, Madeleine Albright, Boutros Boutros-Ghali, economists such as Alan Greenspan and Milton Friedman, and writers such as Jack Kerouac, Allen Ginsberg, Federico García Lorca, J.D. Salinger, Isaac Asimov and Paul Auster. Columbia University today has more than 24000 students. Visitors may walk freely around campus. The main buildings are spread around a vast plaza. To the north, **Low Memorial Library**★ (1895) is reminiscent of Rome's Pantheon. Its interior staircase is dominated by a statue of the goddess Minerva. Inside, you can admire the rotunda and the Beaux-Arts style décor. The brick **Earl Hall** (1902), topped with a cupola, is distinguishable by its pediment and Neoclassical

columns. It houses the social services center and the center of religious confessions on campus. **St Paul's Chapel** is a church built in brick in Italian Renaissance style, which today hosts concerts. The basement of the **Postcrypt Coffeehouse** rings with memories of the 1960s and the poems of Jack Kerouac and Bob Dylan songs. On the south side of the chapel, you'll find **Buell Hall** (1878) and all that remains of the psychiatric asylum that occupied this site before the university. The Maison Française, the cultural center of the university, is installed on the floor above. Behind, a bronze reproduction of the *Penseur* by Rodin marks the entrance to the philosophy and French building. The **Butler Library** (1934) houses the campus library, one of the largest in the country: here are more than 2 million of the university's 9.2-million volume collection.

RIVERSIDE DRIVE AND PARK★★

D1-2/C2-3 The park spreads out on the riverside (as the name suggests), along **Riverside Drive**, from 72nd to 155th Sts. The most pleasant section is situated to the south of 100th St; be sure to stop at the **garden and crabapple grove** (91st St.).

RIVERSIDE CHURCH★★

D1 Riverside Dr. and 120th St. - www.trcnyc.org - 9am-5pm.
This imposing Neo-Gothic church, with its 120m/394ft bell tower, was partially financed by John D. Rockefeller. Its east portal is inspired by Chartres Cathedral in France. Inside you'll find two stained glass panels from the 16C, from the cathedral in Bruges and a chiming clock made up of 74 bells.

GENERAL GRANT NATIONAL MEMORIAL★

D1 Riverside Dr. (facing the church, at the level of 122nd St.) - $\wp$ 212 666 1640 - www.nps.gov/gegr - welcome centre: daily except Mon-Tue 9am-5pm; mausoleum : daily except Mon-Tue 10am-11am, 12pm-1pm, 2pm-3pm and 4pm-5pm - closed Thanksgiving and Dec 25 - free.
This monument (1896) is dedicated to **Ulysses S. Grant**, president of the United States from 1869 to 1877. A vast dome covers the crypt in which niches house busts of Grant's comrades in arms. Photographs arranged across two small rooms tell the story of his life.

---

*In 2016, the **Roy and Diana Vagelos Education Center**, dedicated to medicine, was inaugurated. Conceived by architectural agency Diller Scofidio + Renfro (responsible for the famous High Line), the 14-story building comprises a structure mixing steel and concrete, inside which the study rooms combine with a vertical circulation, named a "study cascade". Haven Ave., corner of W. 171st St.*

Harlem ★

Harlem is a neighborhood of juxtapositions, with its handsome brownstones, cocktail bars, and upscale restaurants alongside crumbling public housing projects (council housing) and pockets of poverty. With Columbia University directly south and Upper West Side real estate prices driving people north, plus enticing museums and parks, Harlem gentrified rapidly and became a very desirable place to live.

▶**Access:** Subway: 125th and 135th Sts on lines A, B, C, D, 2 and 3. Bus: M1, M7, M10, M11.

Detachable map F1, E1-2.

▶**Tip:** Unless you are going to a gospel service on Sunday (come early, as space is limited), weekdays are more lively. Plan an evening in a jazz club. If you're out quite late, it's easiest to take a cab home. 👍*Our top picks/Nightlife in Harlem, p. 126.*

After the 1658 foundation of the first Dutch village (south of present-day Harlem), the surrounding area remained rural until the arrival of the railway in 1837 and then the overground subway line. Harlem is a historically black neighborhood, although real estate developers initially tried to bring in white tenants. In the 1920s, there were 60 000 black residents in Harlem, which led to some white flight and the beginnings of the area as a hub of black American culture. The birth of **jazz culture** and Prohibition made the lively clubs of Harlem the rendezvous spots of intellectuals, artists and party-makers. The fashionable bars vibrated with the sounds of jazz and blues. This was the golden age of Harlem, with the emergence of a distinct African-American identity. The end of Prohibition and the **Great Depression** (late 1929-1939) would

sound the death knell for this period. The jazz scene would move down to Greenwich Village, while the middle classes were beset by unemployment and left the area, leaving it to be occupied by a more disadvantaged population. The ensuing degradation and extreme poverty in the area meant it subsequently acquired a bleak reputation as a dangerous place. During the 1960s, the raising of black political consciousness would cast Harlem in the spotlight once more, due in part to the passionate political speeches delivered by **Malcolm X** in the Black Muslim Temple of Islam (he was assassinated in 1965 on 166th St). Harlem gave New York its first black mayor, David Dinkins. Slowly at first and then more quickly, the area was built up: new shops started opening, new apartment towers went up, and the historic brownstones were renovated and restored. The neighborhood has retained a strong black identity, but with rents and housing prices increasing, first just a bit and then dramatically, many lower income residents moved and continue to move to less costly neighborhoods in other boroughs.

STUDIO MUSEUM IN HARLEM★

E1 *144 West 125th St. - ☏ 212 864 4500 - www.studiomuseum.org - Thur-Fri 12pm-9pm, Sat 10am-6pm, Sun 12pm-6pm - closed public holidays- $7 (seniors and students $3), free Sundays.*
Since 1968, this museum, dedicated to Afro-American and other local artists, has held fine temporary exhibitions, ranging from folk art to video and more conceptual installations.

MARCUS GARVEY PARK★

F1-2 Heading south, between West 124th and 119th Sts, you'll walk the length of this steep and pretty park. On the west side, you'll see a row of well renovated brownstones, allowing you to imagine the bourgeois Harlem of the end of the 19C.

APOLLO THEATER★

E1 *253 West 125th St. (between Frederick Douglass and Adam Clayton Powell Blvds) - www.apollotheater.org.*
In 1914, this historical icon of jazz did not permit black people to enter. In 1934, it took its present-day name, becoming a temple of black music

and welcoming Louis Armstrong, Aretha Franklin, Ray Charles, James Brown and even The Jackson 5. The Amateur Night (Wednesday) has been the starting place of huge talents. Renovated in 2002, the Apollo has once more become one of the hottest venues in town.

SCHOMBURG CENTER FOR RESEARCH IN BLACK CULTURE★

F1 *515 Malcolm X Blvd (near West 135th St.) - ☏ 212 491 2200 - www.nypl.org - daily except Sun 10am-6pm.*
The Puerto Rican **Arthur Schomburg** (1874-1938) amassed a collection of documents and artifacts that told the story of Afro-American history, heritage and identity. This center gathers more than 5 million documents illustrating black culture

STRIVERS ROW

F1 *West 138th and 139th Sts.*
These beautiful brownstones are where the rising black bourgeoisie of the 1920s lived in Georgian and Neo-Renaissance style residences.

MORRIS-JUMEL MANSION

Off map (by E1) *Corner of W. 160th St. and Edgecombe Ave. - ☏ 212 923 8008 - www.morrisjumel.org - Tue-Fri 10am-4pm, Sat-Sun 10am-5pm - closed Mon & public holidays - $10 (seniors and students $8, under 12s free).*

Apollo Theater

This manor house (1765) is the last testament of the Pre-Revolutionary Period. During the War of Independence (1776), it would house the headquarters of **George Washington**. The Federal style house was bought by the **Jumels**, rich French traders.

HISPANIC SOCIETY OF AMERICA★

Off map (by E1) *613 W 155th St. - ☎ 212 926 2234 - www.hispanic society.org - currently closed for renovation.*
This little museum offers a fascinating look at Hispanic civilization going back to the Pre-Roman era and houses a rich collection of master works. The gallery on the ground floor contains an impressive selection of traditional and ritual objects, pieces of silverware, prehistoric tools, Renaissance recumbent statues and spun fabrics. To the right, don't miss the room dedicated to **Joaquín Sorolla y Bastida** (1863-1923): here you'll find 14 monumental paintings executed between 1911 and 1919 illustrating Spanish traditions and customs.
The **upper gallery** exhibits a fine collection of ceramics, pottery and jewelry and is decorated with a number of **portraits** by Le Greco, Morales, Ribera, Vélasquez and Goya.

93

The Cloisters★★★

Perched on a hill dominating the banks of the Hudson, north of Washington Heights, this museum reproduces the architecture of a fortified European monastery. Inside, the medieval art collection is set amid cloisters dismantled on the Old Continent and reconstructed here in New York. The serene complex displays the art of the Middle Ages to admirable effect.

▶**Access:** Subway: 190th St (followed by 10 min. walk or bus M4)
Fort Tryon Park – 𝒫 212 923 3700 - www.metmuseum.org - March-Oct: 10am-5.15pm (4.45pm Nov-Feb, 7.30pm June-Aug) - closed 1 Jan, Thanksgiving and 25 Dec - $25 combination ticket w/Met (₺ *p. 74*) and Met Breuer (₺ *p. 72*). ***Detachable map. off map around E1.***
▶**Tip:** A great spot for a picnic. Allow 1-1hr30min for the visit.

THE CLOISTERS★★

During his travels, sculptor **George Barnard** collected architectural vestiges of the south of France. In 1925, **John D. Rockefeller** donated sufficient money to the Metropolitan Museum to acquire this collection, to which he would add more works. He then constructed a museum of the Middle Ages in Tryon Park (1938). **Roman art** is showcased in the Romanesque Hall and in *The Fuentidueña Apse* (Castille, 1160). The *Saint-Guilhem Cloister* (Hérault, end of the 12C) is an example from the very origins of Gothic architecture. **Gothic art** can be appreciated in its full splendor with *Langon Chapel* (Moutiers-Saint-Jean Abbey, 13C), the *Abbey of Saint-Michel-de-Cuxa* and the *Chapter House from Notre-Dame-de-Pontaut*. On the lower level, a Gothic chapel houses the tombs of Catalogne et d'Aragon (13-14C). The *Bonnefont Cloister* (France, 13-14C) sits next to a medieval garden opening onto the Hudson. The *Cloister from Trie-en-Bigorre* (end of 15C) evokes the contemplative atmosphere of a monastery.

THE COLLECTIONS★★★

The **Glass Gallery** brings together a series of stained glass windows, statues and a Flemish altarpiece depicting the Nativity (Rogier Van der Weyden, 15C). The **treasury** brings together a collection of sacred objects: *cloisonné* enamel from Limoges (13C), Rosary beads (Holland, 16C), embroidered tapestries, illuminated manuscripts of *Riches Heures du duc de Berry*, golden pedestal salt cellars and rock crystal (Paris, 13C). The collection of **tapestries** contains some of the oldest in the world (15-16C), including *The Hunt of the Unicorn*, from the Château de Verteuil-sur-Charente. Further rooms house stained glass, altarpieces and Gothic statues, as well as the Annunciation Triptych, by Flemish master Robert Campin (15C).

Brooklyn★★ and Queens★

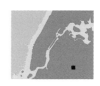

Brooklyn is much larger than Manhattan, so much so that if not part of NYC, it would be the US's fourth-largest city. It's a curious mix of ultra hip, chic and working-class. Each neighborhood offers something a little different: Dumbo is lofts, luxury towers, and Manhattan skyline views, Williamsburg is the seat of bobos, Park Slope is familial, Red Hook quiet and full of warehouses but rapidly becoming popular. North of Brooklyn, Queens is the true American melting pot; more than half of Queens residents speak a language other than English. This is where cinema was born, where new museums are opening and where artists are moving in.

▶**Access:** Almost all subway lines go to Brooklyn and Queens. The numbers of the bus lines that serve Brooklyn are preceded by B, Q for Queens. To get around Queens, take buses or subway lines E, G, N, R and 7. Brooklyn and Queens both have ferry ports (www.ferry.nyc) - one-way $2.75, free transfer available).

Area map p. 96. *Detachable map BC8*, *F4*, *E5-7-8*, *G5*.

▶**Tip:** If you have time, get up early, or stay up late, and cross the Brooklyn Bridge on foot.

BROOKLYN★★

Brooklyn's history goes almost as far back as that of Manhattan. This once rural area was made part of New York in 1898. Today it is the most populated of New York's boroughs (almost 2.6 million inhabitants), with a mix of people and styles. It's a **multicultural** place, shaped by the historical installation of immigrant communities, and also houses a number of trendy, upscale areas, such as **Brooklyn Heights**.
On sunny days, the lawns of **Prospect Park** and the beaches of

Coney Island, to the south, are packed with New Yorkers seeking a little vitamin D.

BROOKLYN HEIGHTS★★

At the time of the American Revolution, this part of Brooklyn served as the headquarters for **George Washington**. Subsequently it became the first area to be developed when transfers to Manhattan became easier. The **promenade**, which overlooks the river, offers a beautiful **view★★★** over Lower Manhattan and its skyscrapers.

WILLIAMSBURG★

E7-8 Williamsburg is the hip shop window of Brooklyn, originally the haven of artists driven out of Manhattan by skyrocketing prices. The reputation of the area and its laid-back cool vibe, which has now been well and truly cultivated, has made it so desirable that prices have gone through the roof, and the idea of it being an artistic sanctuary is no more than an illusion.

Head there on the weekend, when flea markets enliven the area, attracting a steady stream of young tattooed types in flannel shirts, would-be models and entertained onlookers taking in the open-air fashion show. Turn onto Bedford Ave. and Berry Street, north of the **Williamsburg Bridge**. From this bridge (walk or cycle across) linking the Lower East Side to Brooklyn and the banks of the East River, you can enjoy a fine view of Midtown.

DUMBO★/EMPIRE FULTON FERRY STATE PARK★★

Situated between Brooklyn and Manhattan Bridges, **Dumbo** *(Down Under the Manhattan Bridge Overpass)* is a former warehouse and factory district that changed rapidly in the early 2000s, taken over by young professionals and families. From **Empire Fulton Ferry Park★★** situated on the riverside (often called Brooklyn Bridge Park), you can admire the unforgettable vista of the towers of Manhattan.

PROSPECT PARK★

Three entrances: 150 Eastern Parkway, 455 Flatbush Ave., 990 Washington Ave. - www.prospectpark.org. This green space, designed by the architects and landscapers of Central Park, features stretches of grass and groves, with a more bucolic, rustic feel than its big brother. During summer many concerts are performed here.

Brooklyn Botanic Garden★ - *Lefferts Historic House - www.bbg.org - Mar-Oct, Tue-Fri 8am-6pm, Sat-Sun 10am-6pm; Nov, Tue-Fri 8am-4.30pm, Sat-Sun 10am-4.30pm; Dec-Feb, 10am-4.30pm - $15 (free Thur, Sat morning; Sat-Sun Dec-Mar), $25 combined ticket with the Brooklyn Museum of Art.* Laid out inside the park, this zoo houses around 400 animals from around the world (more than 125 species) and a small 18C Dutch farm.

BROOKLYN MUSEUM OF ART★★

200 Eastern Parkway - ✆ 718 638 5000 - www.brooklynmuseum.org - Wed and Sun 11am-6pm, Thur 11am-10pm, Fri-Sat 11am-8pm - closed Mon-Tue and Jan 1, Thanksgiving and Dec 25 - pay what you wish - suggested admission $16 (seniors and students $10, under 18s free); $25 combined ticket with Botanic Garden (seniors and students $16). The Brooklyn Museum (1897) has one of the richest collections in the city. Its works, spread over

Brooklyn by Union Street

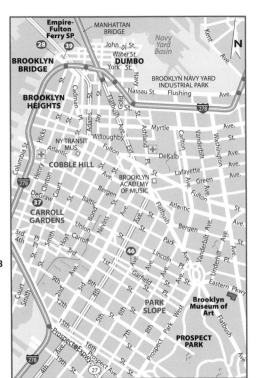

BROOKLYN

```
0        3/10 mi
├────────┤
0        600m
```

WHERE TO EAT

Al di La..............................	**46**
Grimaldi's..........................	**39**
River Café.........................	**28**

WHERE TO DRINK

Brooklyn Farmacy & Soda Fountain.......	**37**

Also see Williamsburg on the detachable map.

52 000 m²/559723 ft², (the museum's whole collection comprises 1.5 million pieces) are of the highest caliber. Their temporary exhibitions are some of the best in town. Unless you want to limit your visit to one particular theme, start on the 5th floor.

American painting and sculpture★★★ – *5ᵗʰ floor*. The key themes in this series of works are the geography, ethnicities and everyday life of the country. Here you'll find landscape paintings, genre paintings, depictions of the War of Secession, exoticism, self-taught painters, artists from the great art schools, the passage from the romantic 19C to the industrial 20C, abstract expressionism, and the minimalism of the second half of the 20C.

Decorative arts★★ – *4ᵗʰ floor*. Here you'll find reconstitutions of interiors in different styles and from different eras, the oldest being a Dutch interior from the 17C. You will also see the eclecticism that marked the end of the 19C and start of the 20C, from the Neo-Gothic to Japanese influence, followed by Arts & Craft, Art Nouveau, and then Art Deco.

Elizabeth A. Sackler Center for Feminist Art★ – 4th floor.
This original department focuses on art seen and made by women on their own terms. The central work is **The Dinner Party**★★ (1974-1979), a vast and impressive installation by Judy Chicago.

Egyptian antiquities★★★ – 3rd floor.
These collections, among the most reputable in the world, bring together fascinating everyday objects. The first part presents the history, with the second explaining the different facets of daily life in Egypt during Antiquity.

European painting★★ – 3rd floor.
This part of the exhibit, laid out around the arcaded cloister, is a walk through 700 years of European painting, including landscapes, portraits and historical or genre scenes, from artists such as Monet, Courbet and Sorolla.

Art from Asia and the Islamic World ★ – 2nd floor.
The arts of various Asian civilizations are on display here (China, Korea, Japan, India, Nepal, and general Southeast Asia) and Arabic (Islamic Art). The 1st floor is dedicated to temporary exhibitions and houses pricey restaurant *The Norm*.

QUEENS★

The most spread out of the five boroughs of New York, Queens, along with Brooklyn, occupies the west part of Long Island. This is where we find two of New York's three airports : JFK and LaGuardia. This is also the home of two of the city's sporting temples, Citi Field and Flushing Meadows, which hosts the US Open Tennis. In the 1920s, the Astoria district was home to around 20 film studios. Today, after having long been disdained, multicultural Queens is turning the explosion of prices in Manhattan to its advantage, attracting artists, young creators, businesses and visitors, the latter who come for its fascinating museums.

MOMA PS1★

E5 22-25 Jackson Ave. (angle 46th Ave.) - ☏ 718 784 2084 - http://momaps1.org - daily except Tue & Wed 12pm-6pm - closed 1 Jan Thanksgiving and 25 Dec - pay what you wish - $10 suggested admission - free (except temporary exhibitions) with MoMA ticket from the last 14 days. Food on site.
This artistic center, dedicated to contemporary art, is part of MoMA, working in conjunction as an incubator for young artists. Housed in a former school constructed in Neo-Renaissance style at the start of the 1890s, it has retained its sombre shell. The contrast is striking between the austerity of the brick walls, endless corridors, and preserved school furniture and the audacity of

the exhibitions presented between the walls of the old classrooms. You'll find paintings featuring distorted bodies, audacious installations and unsettling abstract conceptual videos: it is hard to find a common thread, but impossible not to have some kind of reaction to this fairly exhaustive spread of contemporary art today. The future stars of the MoMA may well be among the exhibited artists.

AMERICAN MUSEUM OF THE MOVING IMAGE★★

G5 36-01 35ᵗʰ Ave. (corner of 36ᵗʰ St.) - Astoria - ☏ 718 777 6888 - www.movingimage.us - Wed-Thur 10.30am-5pm, Fri 10.30am-8pm, Sat-Sun 10.30am-6pm - closed Mon-Tue - $15 (seniors and students $11, 3-17 years $7); free Fri 4pm-8pm - ticket gives access to exhibits and daily screenings.

This museum, featuring costumes and photographs of legendary actors, is located in the former film industry district, on the site of Astoria Studios. Various photos tell the story of the golden age of the studios, but it is above all the permanent exhibit *Behind the Screen* that will enthral children, teens and adults alike. In the immaculately white rooms, you'll find close to 130 000 nostalgia-inducing objects (cameras, décor, costumes, wigs, etc.), from the Chewbacca costume in *Star Wars* to the scary

mannequin of *The Exorcist*. Early arcade games are exhibited (including the legendary *Tron*) and a cinema revisiting Ancient Egypt is recreated. Interaction is built in to the exhibits, with the opportunity to try your hand at the techniques of dubbing, making your own animated film, or even creating the soundtrack of a Hollywood blockbuster. A fascinating and educational visit, great fun for kids and adults.

NOGUCHI MUSEUM★

F4 9-01 33ʳᵈ Rd., Long Island City - ☏ 718 204 7088 - www.noguchi.org - daily except Mon & Tue 10am-5pm (until 8pm 1ˢᵗ Fri of the month May-Sept), Sat-Sun 11am-6pm - closed Jan 1, Thanksgiving and Dec 25. - $10 (seniors and students $5); free 1st Fri of the month.

Isamu Noguchi (1904-1988), a great American sculptor of Japanese origin, Noguchi is famous for his gardens (UNESCO, Paris), his public spaces (Hart Plaza, Detroit), his playgrounds (Playscape, Atlanta), his objects (the famous paper and bamboo Akari lamps) and his theater sets (Balanchine, Martha Graham). The museum presents samples of his sculptures, as well as the sculptures of other contemporary artists. It also organizes a roster of photography and design exhibitions.

Addresses

Smith & Mills
© Paul Wagtouicz/Smith & Mills

🍴

Where to eat

At any hour of the day, you can find something inexpensive to eat, even in the most upscale districts (for a picnic, almost any supermarket is a good bet). You will never be short on restaurant choices. On the weekends, do as New Yorkers do and indulge in brunch. ⚭ *Where to drink p. 112 and Eating out p. 138.*

⚭ *Find the addresses on our maps using the numbers in the listing (ex. ①). The coordinates in red (ex. C2) refer to the detachable map (inside the cover).*

104 LOWER MANHATTAN

Area map p. 16-17

Around $ 20

⑬ Adrienne's Pizzabar – *A8* - *54 Stone St. - Ⓜ Wall St. - ☏ 212 248 3838 - www.adriennespizzabarnyc. com - 11.30am-12am, Sun 11am,-10pm - closed Thanksgiving and 25 Dec - mains $17/$122.* Delicious pizzas as well as oven dishes and salads.

From $20 to $40

⑩ Pier A Harbor House – *A8* - *22 Battery Pl. - Ⓜ Bowling Green - ☏ 212 785 0153 - www.piera.com - ♿ - Mon-Wed 11am-2am, Thur-Sat 11am-4am, Sun 11am-12am - mains $16/$36.* Perched on the edge of the Hudson, this historic establishment converted into a restaurant features a large terrace with uninterrupted views of the movements of the boats and the Statue of Liberty. Expect great seafood, including an excellent *mi-cuit* tuna burger and a tasty fish & chips.

CHINATOWN

Area map p. 31

From $30 to $50

㉕ Peking Duck House – *B7* - *28 Mott St. - between Chatham Sq. and Pell St. - Ⓜ Canal St. - ☏ 212 227 1810 - www.pekingduckhousenyc.com - ♿ - 11.3am-10.30-pm, Fri-Sat 11.45am-11pm - mains $35/$44.* The crispy-skinned Peking duck ($54) wrapped in pancakes is a treat not to be missed.

NOLITA

Area map p. 36

Less than $20

⑰ Lovely Day – *B7* - *196 Elizabeth St. - Ⓜ Bowery - ☏ 212 925 3310 - www.lovelydaynyc.com - Sun-Thur 11am-11pm, Fri-Sat 11am-12am - mains $8/$17.* Floral wallpaper, red moleskin banquettes and stools and a vintage tile floor look more diner than Thai, but the Thai food here is superb.

From $20 to $30

㉑ Mottsu – *B7* - *285 Mott St. - between Houston and Prince Sts - Ⓜ Prince St. - ☏ 212 343 8017 - www. mottsu.com - 11.30am-11pm, Fri 11h.30am-11.30pm, Sat 12.30pm*

-11.30pm, Sun 12.30pm-11pm - mains $11/$26. Excellent Japanese food. Expect maki, sushi and other fish-based dishes.

SOHO

Area map p. 31

Up to $20
5 Dean & Deluca – *B7* - 560 Broadway St. - corner of Prince St. - Ⓜ Prince St - ☏ 212 226 6800 - www.deandeluca.com - Mon-Fri 7am-9pm, Sat-Sun 8am-9pm. Pricey gourmet shop with stalls overspilling with top-shelf produce, cheeses and condiments. Good for upscale food gifts or picnic fare.

From $30 to $50
12 Giorgione – *A7* - 307 Spring St. - Ⓜ Spring St. - ☏ 212 352 2269 - www.giorgionenyc.com - 🅿 ♿ - 12pm-11pm - closed Sun - $9/$36. Expect a relaxed atmosphere in this Italian restaurant offering delightful pasta, pizza and espresso.

48 Troquet – *B7* - 155 Grand St. - Ⓜ Canal St. - ☏ 212 343 4295 - 11.30am-1am - lunch $19/$25, around $30/$45 for evening à la carte. Behind Troquet is the story of a group of friends with a dream of New York; this includes the chef Camille Martin, who previously presided over kitchens in Sri Lanka, under the aegis of the Pourcel brothers. In this cute, hip Parisian-bistro-style establishment, you'll find well-executed Franco-American cuisine accompanied by a fine wine menu and rounded off with a warm, inviting atmosphere.

☺ **41 Racines – *B7*** - 94 Chambers St. - Ⓜ Chambers St. - ☏ 212 227 3400 - racinesnewyork.azurewebsites.net - 6pm-10.30pm - closed Sun - mains $24/ $44. A long, brick-walled leads to a kitchen where chef David Duca (hailing from Marseilles, and Michelin star-winning in Paris) creates remarkable offerings. Expect well-balanced and technical dishes using the best fresh American produce (seafood from Maine, lamb from Colorado, vegetables from Oregon). Polite and assured service from the largely French team. Low-key atmosphere. A real treat.

LOWER EAST SIDE

Area map p. 36   105

From $20 to $40
29 Russ & Daughters – *C7* - 179 East Houston St. - Ⓜ 2nd Ave. - ☏ 212 475 4880 - www.russanddaughters.com - 8am-8pm, Sat 8am-7pm, Sun 8am 5.30pm - mains $12/$24. Loyal customers come here for the chewy bagels, extra-creamy cream cheese and salmon or other smoked fish.

11 Freemans – *B7* - 191 Chrystie St. - Freeman Alley - Ⓜ Bowery - ☏ 212 420 0012 - www.freemansrestaurant.com - ♿ - 11am-11.30pm, Sat-Sun 10am-11.30pm - mains $18/$33. This restaurant, decorated in the style of a country hunting lodge, serves great rustic dishes.

🍴

GREENWICH VILLAGE

Area map p. 41

Up to $20

9 **Corner Bistro** – *B6* - *331 West 4th St. - angle Jane St. -* Ⓜ *Bleecker St. - ☎ 212 242 9502 - www.cornerbistrony. com - 11.30am-4am, Sun 12pm-4am - closed Thanksgiving & 25 Dec - dishes less than $20.* Long a favorite for burger lover in the city and among the cheapest.

43 **Umami Burger** – *B6* - *432 6th Ave -* Ⓜ *14th St. - ☎ 212 677 8626 - www. umamiburger.com - Sun-Wed 11.30am -11pm, Fri-Sat 11.30am-12am -dishes less than $20.* A good Californian chain in NYC. Here you can enjoy a great burger. Quality products are used (special mention to the chunks of lard that replace bacon).

106

44 **Ancolie** – *B6* - *58 W 8th St. -* Ⓜ *9th St. - ☎ 646 524 5929 - www. ancolie.com - Mon-Fri 8am-7pm, Sat 9am-7pm, Sun 9am-5pm - dishes less than $20.* Opened by a French woman who left Wall Street to follow her culinary passion, this little establishment offers bowls of salad and freshly made healthy dishes. Tasty desserts. Take-out also available.

From $20 to $40

32 **Frankies Spuntino** – *B6* - *570 Hudson St. -* Ⓜ *Christopher St. - ☎ 212 924 0818 - frankies570.com -* ♿ *- 11am-11pm, Fri-Sat 11.30am-12am - closed 25 Dec - mains $15/$28.* Expect a chic feel and pared-down décor in this Italian restaurant employing simple recipes and high-quality

ingredients. You'll find tasty crostini, excellent grilled calamari and marinated pork. Some great wine (including a Barolo).

☺ 34 **Mary's Fish Camp** – *B6* - *64 Charles St. -* Ⓜ *Christopher St. - ☎ 646 486 2185 - www.marysfish camp.com - 12pm-3pm, 6pm-11pm, Sun 12pm-4pm - mains $15/$32.* Noisy but convivial atmosphere in this restaurant that celebrates seafood from the East Coast, including grilled sea bass, mussels, clams and lobster rolls.

31 **The Spotted Pig** – *B6* - *314 West 11th St. -* Ⓜ *Christopher St. - ☎ 212 620 0393 - www.thespottedpig.com - 12pm-2am, Sat-Sun 11am-2am - closed 25 Dec - mains $20/$39.* This cool, charmingly decorated restaurant serves quality cuisine with an Italian twist. Expect a celeb sighting or two.

EAST VILLAGE

Up to $20

20 **Momofuku Noodle Bar** – *C6* - *171 1st Ave. -* Ⓜ *Astor Pl. -between 10th and 11th St. - ☎ 212 777 7773 - www. momofuku.com - 12pm-11pm, Sat 12pm-1am - mains $13/$17.* Seating along a counter. The menu includes smoked chicken wings, Chinese buns and assorted noodles.

From $20 to $30

1 **B-Bar & Grill** – *C7* - *40 E 4th St. -* Ⓜ *Astor Pl. - ☎ 212 475 2220 - www.bbarandgrill.com - 12pm-12am, Fri 12pm-4am, Sat 11am-4am, Sun 11am-12am - mains $15/$23.* This friendly diner serves a good range of

© Zoran Jelenic/Spotted Pig

Spotted Pig

international cuisine. Large terrace lit by multicolored lanterns.

27 Supper – **C7** - 156 East 2ⁿᵈ St. - Aves A and B - Ⓜ 2ⁿᵈ Ave. - ℘ 212 477 7600 - www.supperrestaurant.com - 🖾 - 4pm-12am, Sat 10am-1am, Sun 10am-12am - closed 25 Dec - mains $18/$25. Décor is understated and warm. Excellent North Italian food. A fine terrace for sunny days.

CHELSEA

Up to $20

45 Bare Burger – 535 LaGuardia Pl. - Ⓜ Bleecker St. - **B6** - ℘ 212 477 8125 - bareburger.com - 11.30am-10.30pm, Sat 11am-11pm- dishes less than $20.

A chain with an excellent reputation for quality, organic food. Expect tasty, juicy burgers and a great selection of craft beers on tap. Multiple locations (see website).

7 Chelsea Market – **B6** - 75 9ᵗʰ Ave - 15ᵗʰ and 16ᵗʰ Sts - Ⓜ 8ᵗʰ Ave. - ℘ 212 652 2110 - www.chelseamarket.com - 7am-9pm, Sun 8am-8pm. Here you'll find all the ingredients for an excellent picnic: fresh or dried fruit, pastries, sandwiches, soups, salads and more. If the weather isn't so great, you can sit here or choose one of the little restaurants. Very busy on weekends.

24 Café Serai – **B6** - 150 West 17ᵗʰ St. - in the Rubin Museum of Art - Ⓜ 18ᵗʰ St. - ℘ 212 620 5000 - www. rubinmuseum.org - 11am-5pm, Wed

🍴

11am-9pm, Fri 11am-10pm, Sat-Sun 11am-6pm - closed Tue, Thanksgiving and 25 Dec - mains $10/$16. Excellent wraps, salads and dishes with a North Indian and Tibetan influence. Don't miss heart *momos* (dumplings).

From $20 to $30

6 **Cookshop** – *B5* - *156 10th Ave. - corner of 20th St. -* Ⓜ *23rd St. (8th Ave.) - ℘ 212 924 4440 - www.cookshop ny.com - 8am-11.30pm, Sat 10am-11.30pm, Sun 10am-10pm - closed 25 Dec - mains $23/$28.* Cuisine made from ingredients brought from producers in the Hudson Valley and in Vermont. The menus and décor offer elegant simplicity.

UNION SQUARE AND MADISON SQUARE

Up to $20

2 **Eisenberg's** – *C6* - *174 5th Ave. - 22nd and 23rd St. -* Ⓜ *23rd St. - ℘ 212 675 5096 - www.eisenbergsnyc.com - 6.30am-8pm, Sat 9am-6pm, Sun 9am-5pm - under $20.* This deli, opened in 1929, has defied fashions and fads, consistently offering generous helpings of substantial, well-executed fare. The setting is unchanging, but the sandwiches are always excellent (especially the pastrami and tuna). An excellent option in this area where it's hard to find good food at modest prices.

From $20 to $30

8 **Eataly** – *C6* - *200 5th Ave. -* Ⓜ *23rd St. - ℘ 212 229 2560 - www.eataly.com - ♿ - 9am-11pm - closed Thanksgiving and 25 Dec.*

A vast temple dedicated to Italian gastronomy: produce, meats, seafood, bread and pastries and several restaurants. Rooftop bar.

47 **abcv** – *C6* - *35 E 18th St. -* Ⓜ *23rd St. - ℘ 212 475 5829 - www.abchome.com/eat/abcv/- 12pm-3pm, 5.30pm-10.30pm (11pm Thur-Sat) - closed Sat lunchtime and Sun - plates $9/$18.* The most recent restaurant of Jean-Georges Vongerichten. Serves flavored food and has a vegetarian menu. Cool interior.

MIDTOWN WEST

Up to $20

35 **Shake Shack** – *C5* - *691 8th Ave. -* Ⓜ *42nd St. - ℘ 646 435 0135 - www.shakeshack.com - 11am-12am - mains less than $20.* A high-end fast food joint from Danny Meyer. If you're craving a hot dog or burger you won't be disappointed (quality brioche buns, well-seasoned meat).

😊 **36** **Kung Fu Little Steamed Buns Ramen** – *C4* - *811 8th Ave. -* Ⓜ *42nd St. - (close to corner of 49th St.) - ℘ 917 388 2555 - www.kungfulittlesteamedbunsramen.com - 10.30am-10pm - dishes less than $20.* Welcome to the kingdom of noodles! Peter Song, the chef who you'll see rolling out and striking the noodle dough behind a glass pane, is a specialist. The noodles are eaten in soups or sautés. Excellent dumplings.

From $30 to $50

22 **Nobu 57** – *CD4* - *40 West 57th St. -* Ⓜ *57th St. - ℘ 212 757 3000 - www.noburestaurants.com - 11.45am-2.15pm, 5.45pn-11.15pm - mains*

© Heather Shimmin/iStockphoto.com

Shake Shack

$33/$42. In a softly-lit, sleek setting, enjoy high-end Japanese cuisine, including the famous miso cod.

MIDTOWN EAST

From $30 to $50
😊 **23** **Oyster Bar** – **C5** - 89 East 42nd St. - Grand Central Terminal - Ⓜ Grand Central - ☏ 212 490 6650 - www.oysterbarny.com - ♿ - 11.30am -9.30pm - closed bank holidays and Sundays - mains $29/$38. An unbeatable Midtown spot for fresh seafood.

CENTRAL PARK

From $20 to $40
3 **The Loeb Boathouse at Central Park** – **D3** - East 72nd St. - Ⓜ 72th St. - ☏ 212 517 2233 - www. thecentralparkboathouse.com - 12pm-9pm, Sat-Sun 9.30am-9.30pm - mains $18/$26. In the heart of Central Park, this romantic restaurant and its veranda offers the best views of the sun setting on the water – and the food is great.

UPPER EAST SIDE

From $20 to $30

18 Maya – *E4* - 1191, 1st Ave. - M Lexington Ave. - ☎ 212 585 1818 - www.richardsandoval.com/mayany - 3pm-10pm, Thur-Fri 3pm-11pm, Sat 11.30am-11pm, Sun 11.30am-10pm - closed 25 and 31 Dec - mains $16/$30. Mexican cuisine, harmoniously blending tradition and contemporary, is a served in a refined but welcoming setting.

UPPER WEST SIDE

Up to $20

37 Whole Foods Market – *C4* - 10 Columbus Circle - on the basement level of the Time Warner Shopping Center - M 59th St. - ☎ 212 823 9600 - 7am-11pm. Quality produce, fruit and veg, cheeses, breads, etc. Eat on the premises or take it to Central Park is just next-door. You'll find themed hot and cold food bars (Indian, Mexican, Japanese) where you can fill up your own containers, buffet-style.

From $30 to $50

14 Isabella's – *D3* - 359 Columbus Ave. - at 77th St. - M 79th St. - ☎ 212 724 2100 - www.isabellas.com - ♿ - 11.30am-10pm, Mon 11.30am -9.30pm, Fri 11.30am-10.30pm, Sat 10am-10.30pm, Sun 10am-9.30pm - mains $24/$39. New American cuisine with touches of Mediterranean, in a relaxed setting. Great terrace and delicious brunch on weekends. Very popular.

From $60 to $240

4 Jean-Georges – *C4* - 1 Central Park West (in Trump Tower) - M 59thSt./Columbus Circle - ☎ 212 299 3900 - jean-georgesrestaurant.com - ♿ - 11.45am-11pm - set menus $58 (lunch)/ $238. Exceptional American cuisine from Michelin triple-starred Jean-Georges Vongerichten, in an exceptionally elegant space. Extremely professional service. The lunch menu offers very good value indeed, with two dishes for less than $60.

BROOKLYN - WILLIAMSBURG

Area map p. 98

Up to $20

39 Grimaldi's – *B8* - 1 Front St. - 11201 Brooklyn - M York St. - ☎ 718 85 84 300 - www.grimaldis-pizza.com - ✖ ♿ - 11.30am-8.30pm - dishes less than $20. Under the Brooklyn Bridge, this restaurant is famous for its pizzas. It's very popular with hungry bridge-walkers, so expect a long line.

40 Meatball Shop – *E7* - 170 Bedford Ave. - 11249 Brooklyn - M Bedford Ave. - ☎ 718 551 0520 - www.themeatballshop.com - 11.30am-2am, Fri-Sat 11.30am-4am - dishes less than $20. The specialty meatballs are juicy and very flavorsome, with sandwich and burger options (veg, too). Multiple locations.

From $20 to $0

😊 **42** **Fette Sau** – *E7* - 354 Metropolitan Ave - Ⓜ Metropolitan Ave. - ☏ 718 963 3404 - www. fettesaubbq.com - 5pm-11pm, Thur & Sun. 12pm-11pm, Fri-Sat 12pm-12am - dishes $22/$38. Expect excellent American barbecue with pork ribs, grilled beef and sausages from heritage breeds raised naturally on small farms. For sides, try the broccoli salad. The vibe is relaxed, featuring big tables, around which diners eat with their hands, in a hangar that opens onto the road.

😊 **49** **The Four Horsemen** – *E7* - 295 Grand St. - Ⓜ Metropolitan Ave. - ☏ 718 599 4900 - fourhorsemenbk. com - 5.30pm-1am, Sat-Sun 1pm-1am - plates $13/$32. The restaurant from the singer James Murphy (of LCD Soundsystem) opened in June 2015, and has been a resounding success. The concept is inventive and modern small plates to share, comprising surf and turf, and an impressive selection of natural wines.

46 **Al Di La** – 248 5th Ave. - Ⓜ Union St. - ☏ 718 783 4565 - www.aldilatrattoria.com - 12pm-3pm, 6pm-10.30pm, Sat-Sun 11am-3.30pm, 5.10pm-11pm (10pm Sun) - mains $19/$29. This *trattoria* is a firm favorite with locals . From the antipasto to the desserts, everything is pitched just right, with distinct and powerful flavors. You'll find pasta is prepared in authentic Italian style, with the choice of more ambitious dishes such as braised rabbit. Great décor with a charming touch of old-fashioned charm.

More than $60

28 **River Café** – *B8* - 1 Water St. - 11201 Brooklyn - Ⓜ York St. - ☏ 718 522 5200 - www.rivercafe.com - Ⓟ on reservation - 8.30am-11.30am, 5.30pm-11pm, Sat 11.30am-2.30pm, Sun 11.30am-2.30pm, 5.20pm-11pm - fixed menu $ 125. Breathtaking view of Manhattan and excellent cuisine. A little stuffy, but there are few other riverfront options. After 4pm, suit jackets obligatory for men and ties preferred.

26 **Peter Luger** – *D8* - 178 Broadway - 11211 Brooklyn - angle Driggs St. - Ⓜ Marcy Ave. - ☏ 718 387 7400 - www.peterluger.com - 🚫 Ⓟ 🚹 - 11.45am-10pm, Fri-Sat 11.45am-10.45pm, Sun 12.45pm-10pm - dishes $51/$97. A carnivore's dream. Reservation essential. Wear loose trousers.

QUEENS

From $20 to $40

38 **Ornella** – *H3* - 29-17 23th Ave. - 11105 Astoria - Ⓜ Astoria Blvd - ☏ 718 777 9477 - www.ornella trattoria.com - 12pm-10pm, Thur-Sat 12pm-11pm - mains $20/$25. A *trattoria* known for the excellent quality of its products (stuffed clams, meatballs, pasta).

Where to drink

New York offers a plethora of cafés, wine bars, bakeries and rooftops. Note that all bars are 21+, but restaurants with bars allow guests of all ages.

♿Find the addresses on our maps using the numbers in the listing (ex. ①). The coordinates in red (ex. C2) refer to the detachable map (inside the cover).

LOWER MANHATTAN

Area map p. 16-17

😀 ① **The Black Tail** – *A8* - Pier A Harbor House - 22 Battery Place (2nd floor) - Ⓜ Bowling Green - ℘ 212 785 0153 - blacktailnyc.com - 5pm-2am - cocktails $16. Playing on the theme of Prohibition in Cuba, this artfully decorated cocktail bar (think wood paneling and soft lighting) has a meticulously put-together list of drinks and a joyful atmosphere: a great spot.

😀 ⑯ **The Dead Rabbit** – *A8* - 30 Water St. - Ⓜ Bowling Green/South Ferry Station - ℘ 646 422 7906 - www.deadrabbitnyc.com - 11am-4am (the cocktail bar, on the 1st floor opens around 5pm) - cocktails $16. This is, according to specialist magazine *Drinks International*, the best cocktail bar in the world. Behind an anonymous looking facade hides the den of two Northern Irish friends, who are revolutionizing the cocktail bar scene. On the ground floor is an authentic Irish tavern (with a suitably long list of whiskeys). Upstairs, mixologists take wicked delight in turning patrons' taste buds upside down.

NOLITA

Area map p. 36

② **Rice to Riches** – *B7* - 37 Spring St. - between Mott and Mulberry Sts - Ⓜ Spring St - ℘ 212 274 0008 - www.ricetoriches.com - 11am-11pm, Fri-Satt 11am-1am. Rice pudding in every flavor and color imaginable.

③ **Café Habana** – *B7* - 17 Prince St. - near Elizabeth St. - Ⓜ Broadway - Lafayette ℘ 212 625 2001 - www.cafehabana.com - 9am-12am. Expect *muy caliente* atmosphere in this Cuban spot where visitors savor cocktails and empanadas.

㉛ **Eileen's** – *B7* - 17 Cleveland Pl. - angle Kenmare and Centre Sts - Ⓜ Spring St. - ℘ 212 966 5585 - www.eileenscheesecake.com - 8am-9pm, Sat-Sun 10am-7pm. The richest, creamiest cheesecakes in dozens of flavors.

TRIBECA - SOHO

Area map p. 31

😀 ㉟ **Grand Banks** – *A7* - Pier 25 - Hudson River Park - Ⓜ Franklin St. - ℘ 212 660 6312 - www.grandbanks.org - Apr-Oct - Mon-Tue 3pm-12am, Wed-Fri 12pm-12am, Sat-Sun 11am-12am. This schooner dating from 1942 is today the city's most popular boat-bar-restaurant serving seafood. The oysters are excellent, but getting a table is near-miraculous, though you can always come for a drink and admire the magnificent view over New Jersey and the skyscrapers of the Financial District. Magic at sunset. The wait can be long.

⑤ Smith & Mills – *A7* - *71 North Moore St. - between Greenwich and Hudson Sts -* Ⓜ *Franklin St. -* ℘ *212 226 2515 - www.smithandmills.com - 11am-2am, Thur-Sat 11am-3am.* With its retro accents and tasty cocktails, this tiny bar is a must.

㉑ Houston Hall – *B6* - *222 W. Houston St. -* Ⓜ *Canal St. -* ℘ *212 675 9323 - www.houstonhallny.com - 4pm-1am, Wed 4pm-2am, Thur 12pm-2am, Fri-Sat. 12pm-3am, Sun 12pm-1am.* This American-scale establishment with exposed brick and beams gives you a lot of bar for your buck. With its huge cask, this bar feels welcoming despite its size (as long as you don't mind crowds and sports screens).

㉕ Macao – *B7* - *311 Church St. -* Ⓜ *Canal St. -* ℘ *212 431 8642 - www.macaonyc.com - 5pm-2am, Thur-Sat 5pm-4am.* This former opium den is something of a New York sensation; the sign and outside appearance contrast with the opulence of the interiors, set across two floors. Décor is a revisit to traditional Chinese aesthetic and the cocktails are creative.

㉗ Pegu Club – *B7* - *77 West Houston St. - W Broadway and Wooster St. -* Ⓜ *Bleecker St. -* ℘ *212 473 7348 - www.peguclub.com - 5pm-2am,* *Fri-Sat 5pm-4am.* Expect intimate ambiance in this long, narrow bar where you'll sip on excellent cocktails (the Champagne concoctions are particularly good). Look out for the discreet entrance: only a little sign announces the place – go through the door and upstairs. Live music on some evenings.

㉜ Azul On The Rooftop – *A7* - *Hotel Hugo (*⚓ *p. 128) - 525 Greenwich St. -* Ⓜ *Spring St. -* ℘ *212 608 4848 - www.azulrooftop.com - Mon-Thur 5pm-11pm, Fri-Sat 4pm-1am, Sun 4pm-11pm.* Not the most spectacular of the rooftops, but it is one of the most secret. Expect soft armchairs, wood paneling and a fun atmosphere with a Cuban twist. Uninterrupted views over the Hudson and Soho.

LOWER EAST SIDE

Area map p. 56

⑥ Dudley's – *C7* - *85 Orchard St - angle Broome St. -* Ⓜ *Delancey St. -* ℘ *212 925 7355 - www.dudleysnyc.com - 9am-2am, Wed-Thur 9am-3am, Fri-Sat 9am-4am, Sun 9am-12am.* Corner bar with long bay windows onto the street, pretty bohemian décor and jazzy soundtracks. Cocktails, beers and (biodynamic) wines, and food served at all hours. Simple and effective.

⑦ Il Laboratorio del Gelato – *C7* - *188 Ludlow St. -* Ⓜ *2nd Ave. -* ℘ *212 343 9922- www.laboratorio delgelato.com - 7.30am-10pm, Fri 7.30am-12am, Sat 10am-12am, Sun 10am-10pm.* A little shop with the creamiest of ice creams gives directly

🍸

on to the "laboratory", where some 75 flavors, spanning the classic to the more experimental, are made.

🍸 **28** **Mr Purple** – *C7* - *171 Ludlow St. -* Ⓜ *2nd Ave. -* ✆ *212 237 1790 - www.hotelindigolowereastside.com - 4pm-2am, Wed 4pm-3am, Thur-Fri 4pm-4am, Sat 11am-4am, Sun 11am-2am.* The rooftop of Hotel Indigo is one of the city's newest. Located on the 15th floor, it offers a 360° view over the city. Patrons can choose to stay sheltered behind the glass bay window and enjoy the sparkle of the Manhattan skyscrapers, or head on to the terrace, in front of the (largely decorative) heated pool, sipping on beautifully crafted cocktails.

GREENWICH VILLAGE

Area map p. 41

8 **Magnolia Bakery** – *B6* - *401 Bleecker St. -* Ⓜ *Bleecker St. -* ✆ *212 462 2572 - www.magnolia bakery.com - 9am-11.30pm, Fri-Sat 9am-12.30am - closed Thanksgiving and 25 Dec.* This bakery that was immortalized by *Sex and the City* sells cupcakes, cheesecakes and other delicious desserts.

9 **Caffe Vivaldi** – *B6* - *32 Jones St. -* Ⓜ *West 4th St. -* ✆ *212 691 7538 - www.caffevivaldi.com - 6pm-11.30pm, Fri 5pm-12am, Sat 6pm-12am.* Calm and cozy bar dedicated to classical music and jazz. A good spot to stop for a cake or panini.

EAST VILLAGE

Area map p. 36

10 **Mudspot** – *C6* - *307 East 9th St. -* Ⓜ *Astor Pl. -* ✆ *212 529 8766 - www.mudnyc.com - 7.30am-12am, Sat-Sun 8am-12am.* Great little all-hours café, which is a good spot for brunch, a snack or evening drink.

22 **Ten Degrees** – *C7* - *121 St. Marks Pl. -* ✆ *212 358 8600 - www.10degreesbar.com - 12pm-4am.* Hip wine (and cocktail). The décor is very of-the-moment with wood cabinets, brick walls and salvaged pieces. From 12-8pm, drinks are two for the price of one. Charcuterie and cheese boards available.

12 **Anyway Café** – *C7* - *34 East 2nd St. - between Bowery and 2nd Ave. -* Ⓜ *2nd Ave. -* ✆ *212 533 3412 - www. anywaycafe.com - 12pm-2am, Fri-Sat 12pm-4am.* On a quiet side street, patrons here sip on vodka while nibbling on blinis.

CHELSEA/MEATPACKING

Area map p. 41

🍸 **36** **The Top of The Standard** – *B6* - *848 Washington St. -* ✆ *212 645 4646 -* Ⓜ *8th Ave. - www.standard hotels.com -* ♿ *- 4pm-4am.* The panoramic bar of The Standard hotel is one of the most popular in New York. Chic interiors with stripped-back design. You must have a drink on the terrace at sunset, taking in the magnificent view. In the evening, access is often restricted to celebrities and VIPs; very crowded on weekends.

UNION SQUARE AND MADISON SQUARE

㉖ 230 Fifth – *C5* - 230 5th Ave. - proche W 27th St. - Ⓜ *Union Square -* 🎧 212 725 4300 - www.230-fifth.com - ♿ - 4pm-4am, Sat 10am-4am, Sun 10am-12am. A rooftop recommended for its impressive view of Empire State Building and the skyscrapers of Midtown. Great for weekday happy hour on a warm, sunny evening.

⑬ City Bakery – *B6* - 3 West 18th St. - 5th and 6th Aves. - Ⓜ *Union Square -* 🎧 212 366 1414 - www.thecitybakery. com - 7.30am-7pm, Sat 8am-7pm, Sun 9am-6pm. One of the best-reputed bakeries in the city, great for a sweets pitstop or a more substantial snack.

⑭ Max Brenner – *C6* - 841 Broadway - 13th and 14th Sts. - Ⓜ *Union Square -* 🎧 646 467 8803 - www. maxbrenner.com - 9am-12am, Fri-Sat 9am-1am, Sun 9am-11pm. Pots filled with steaming concoctions and a menu of almost exclusively chocolate-based treats.

😊 ㉓ Lillies – *C6* - 13 17th St. - 🎧 212 337 1970 - www.lilliesnyc.com - ♿ - 11am-4am - closed 25 Dec. Expect old-fashioned windows, wood paneling, antiques, a monumental fireplace, ornate hanging lanterns and a marble counter. It's Victorian elegance with an undeniably contemporary indie rock soundtrack.

㉙ Old Town Bar – *C6* - 45 East 18th St. - Ⓜ *Union Square -* 🎧 212 529 6732 - www.oldtownbar.com - 11.30am-11.30pm, Sat 12pm-11.30pm, Sun 12pm-10pm. This old school bar, one of the oldest in the city, has been

entertaining its clients since 1882. In the image of the most beautiful English pubs, it has real soul with its wood paneling, mirrors and old-fashioned light fixtures.

MIDTOWN WEST

⑮ Sarabeth's – *D4* - 40 Central Park South - 5th and 6th Aves. - Ⓜ *5th Ave. -* 🎧 212 8265 959 - www.sarabethsrestaurants.com - 🅿 ♿ - 8am-11pm - closed 25 Dec. Ideal for a breakfast or cake stop near Central Park. The pastries are exquisite.

㉞ Bar 54 – *C5* - Hotel Hyatt Centric Times Square New York - 135 W 45th St. - Ⓜ *47-50 Sts.-Rockefeller Center Station -* 🎧 646 364 1234 - https://timessquare.centric.hyatt.com - Sun-Wed 4pm-1am, Thur-Sat 4pm-2am. Funky music and a 1970s atmosphere reign in the city's highest rooftop bar. Magical views of the colorful illuminated skyscrapers of the city (special mention for the view of the Chrysler Building). Impressively, the heaving city down below seems silent from here.

UPPER EAST SIDE

⑰ Dylan's Candy Bar – *D4* - 1011 3rd Ave. - corner of 60th St. - Ⓜ *59th St. -* 🎧 646 735 0078 - www. dylanscandybar.com - 10am-9pm, Fri-Sat 10am-11pm, Sun 11am-9pm - closed Thanksgiving and 25 Dec. In this spot serving milkshakes, candy, and all things sugary, it's hard to resist the treats on offer, whatever your age.

18 **Serendipity 3** – *D4* - *225 East 60th St. - 2nd and 3rd Aves -* Ⓜ *59th St. -* ✆ *212 838 3531 - www.serendipity3. com - 11.30am-12am, Fri-Sat 11.30am -1am.* Kitsch décor in this café-tea room, which is also a restaurant. Kids love it.

19 **Café Sabarsky at the Neue Galerie** – *E3* - *1048 5th Ave. -* Ⓜ *86th St. -* ✆ *212 288 0665 - www.neuegalerie.org - 9am-6pm - closed Tue.* The Museum's elegant Viennese café serves delicious pastries in a refined atmosphere befitting the handsome space.

UPPER WEST SIDE

20 **Hungarian Pastry Shop** – *D2* - *1030 Amsterdam Ave. - 111th St. -* Ⓜ *Cathedral Parkway -* ✆ *212 866 4230 - 8am-11pm, Sat-Sun 8.30am -11pm.* Opposite the Cathedral of Saint John the Divine, this friendly Hungarian café has been used by a number of filmmakers and has a loyal neighborhood following.

BROOKLYN - WILLIAMSBURG

Area map p. 98

24 **The Ides Bar** – *E7* - *80 Wythe Ave. - 11249 Brooklyn -* Ⓜ *Nassau Avenue -* ✆ *718 460 8006 - www. wythehotel.com - 4pm-11pm, Fri 2pm-11pm, Sat-Sun 10am-11pm.* The rooftop of the Wythe Hotel, formerly an enormous warehouse, is a little industrial-vintage gem lined with exposed brick walls. The vibe is relaxed hipsters and cool professionals; superb view over Manhattan.

33 **Westlight** – *E7* - *8111 N 12th St. - 11249 Brooklyn -* Ⓜ *Nassau Ave. -* ✆ *718 307 7100 - westlightnyc.com - Sun-Wed 4pm-12am, Thur-Sat 4pm-2am.* Westlight (on the 22nd floor of the William Vale Hotel) does things big. Expect pretty people, stunning views over Brooklyn and the skyscrapers of Manhattan, a chic yet cozy ambiance and pared-down design. The cocktails are excellent.

30 **Radegast Hall & Biergarten** – *D7* - *113 North 3rd St. -* Ⓜ *Bedford Ave. -* ✆ *718 963 3973 - www.radegast hall.com - 12pm-2am, Fri 12pm-3am, Sat 11am-3am, Sun 11am-2am.* A real *Biergarten*, without the Bavarian folklore. There are two spaces: a dimly-lit wood-lined bar (around which jazz concerts are organized) and a vast room with a retractable roof and long wooden tables. Wide range of beers and food like pretzels and sausages, as well as more surprising options such as *moules-frites*.

37 **Brooklyn Farmacy & Soda Fountain** – *Off map* - *513 Henry St. - corner of Sackett St. -* Ⓜ *Bergen St. -* ✆ *718 522 6260 - www.brooklyn farmacyandsodafountain.com - 8.30am-10pm, Fri. 8.30am-11pm, Sat 10am-11pm, Sun 10am-10pm.* This former pharmacy features apothecary counters where you'll find souvenirs and "made in Brooklyn" gourmet sauces. Specialties of the venue include the sundaes and the egg cream, an ice cream made from chocolate syrup, milk and seltzer. Very popular.

Shopping

Where to buy

For an afternoon of shopping in the department stores, head to Midtown and the Upper East Side. You'll find luxury boutiques on Madison Avenue, on 57th Street and in Soho. Fifth Avenue brings together a range of shops. For hippie and neopunk fashions, head for East Village, Lower East Side, and Williamsburg/Greenpoint. Art galleries and high-end homewares can be found in Chelsea, Soho, Nolita and Tribeca.

What to bring back

New-York themed souvenirs invade tourist shops around Times Square and 5th Avenue. Available in **department stores**, the main American brands offer items only available in the US. The best bargains in fashion and home goods can be found in **specialist outlet stores**, such as Century 21. The **thrift stores** are the best of the best in New York, and dressing in Fifties, Sixties or Eighties vintage fashions is the height of cool in trendy circles. **Sports shops** sell sneakers, American team jerseys and general streetwear.

Museum shops sell posters, models of objects, and art books. Compared to Europe, the prices of **electronics**, are favorable, particularly computers and phones. Don't forget to add the 8.875 % sales tax.

⚷ Find the addresses on our maps using the numbers in the listing (ex. ❶). The coordinates in red (ex. C2) refer to the detachable map (inside the cover).

LOWER MANHATTAN

Area map p. 16-17

❶ **Century 21** – *A8* - *22 Cortlandt St. - Church St. and Broadway -* Ⓜ *Cortland St. - ☎ 212 227 9092 - www.c21stores.com - 7.45am-9pm, Thur-Fri 7.45am-9.30pm, Sat 10am-9pm, Sun 11am-8pm - closed first day of Easter.* A huge store dedicated to discount designer clothing. You will need to rummage, but you can find great bargains.

❸⓪ **Midtown Comics** – *B8* - *64 Fulton St.* - Ⓜ *Fulton St. - ☎ 212 302 8192 - www.midtowncomics.com - 10am-8pm, Wed 8am-8pm, Sat 11am-9pm, Sun 12pm-7pm.* A must for fans of the Marvel universe. You'll find T-shirts and superhero merchandise, but mega-fans will head for the fanzines and first editions.

NOLITA

Area map p. 36

❷ **INA Nolita** – *B7* - *21 Prince St. - Elizabeth St and Mott St* - Ⓜ *Spring St. - ☎ 212 334 9048 - www.inanyc.com - 12pm-8pm, Sun 12pm-7pm.* Luxury thrift store selling womens-wear; garments are little-worn and in good condition; good value.

TRIBECA

Area map p. 31

3 **Philip Williams Posters** – **A7** - 122 Chambers St. - Ⓜ Chambers St. - ℘ 212 513 0313 - postermuseum.com - 10am-7pm - closed Sun and 25 Dec. Old posters of movie stars and legendary brands. Retro and OTT style.

15 **Canal Street Market** – **B7** - 265 Canal St. - Ⓜ Canal St. - canal street market - Mon-Wed 11am-7pm, Thur-Sat 11am-8pm, Sun 11am-6pm (food hall Mon-Sun 10am-8pm). An indoor market dedicated to gastronomy, art, design, fashion and beauty: you'll find 23 themed spaces.

SOHO

Area map p. 31

5 **Prada** – **B7** - 575 Broadway - angle Prince St. - Ⓜ Prince St. - ℘ 212 334 8888 - www.prada.com - 11am-7pm, Sun 11am-6pm. The surreal architecture is the draw here, conceived by Rem Koolhaas. An airy design with a huge curve of wood resembling a skate ramp. This was once the Whitney Museum.

16 **Nike** – **B7** - 529 Broadway - Ⓜ Prince St. - ℘ 646 716 3740 - www.nike.com/us/en_us/retail/en/nike-soho - 10am-8pm. With its giant screens, works from local artists and carefully-curated design, a visit to the famous brand's store is an immersive experience. The highlight is a basketball court on the fifth and final floor, where it's possible to actually test your potential new shoes.

13 **Kith** – **B7** - 644 Broadway - Ⓜ Prince St. - ℘ 646 648 6285 - kith.com - 10am-9pm. A luxury boutique riding the wave of vintage-style sneakers being back in fashion. A number of rare models available. You'll also find quirky items.

6 **Uniqlo** – **B7** - 546 Broadway - near Spring St. - Ⓜ Canal St. - ℘ 877 486 4756 - www.uniqlo.com - 10am-9pm, Sun 11am-8pm. You'll find all the creativity of contemporary Japanese fashion in this low-price store. You'll also find different color variations of cashmere sweaters, impeccably-cut jackets and trousers and artist-designed graphic tees.

LOWER EAST SIDE

Area map p. 36

8 **Economy Candy** – **C7** - 108 Rivington St. - Ludlow and Essex Sts - Ⓜ Essex St. - ℘ 212 254 1531 - www.economycandy.com - 9am-6pm, Mon & Sat. 10am-6pm. Here you'll find shelves upon shelves of candy, chocolate bars and dried fruits, with no-sugar options available.

7 **Shut Skates** – **C7** - 158 Orchard St. - Ⓜ Delancey St. - ℘ 212 420 7488 - www.shutnyc.com - 1pm-7pm. An address that sells only "Made-in-the-US" skateboards. Expect impressive design and quality and well-informed advice.

35 **Tictail Market** – **C7** - 90 Orchard St. - Ⓜ Delancey St. - ℘ 917 388 1556 - tictail.com/tictail-market - 12pm-9pm (Sun until 6pm). Fashion, art and décor are the main events in this boutique, which offers creations from emerging artists from around the world. Chic and tasteful.

GREENWICH VILLAGE

Area map p. 41

⑩ C.O. Bigelow – *B6* - *414 6th Ave. - West 8th and 9th Sts* - Ⓜ *Christopher St.* - ℘ *212 533 2700 - www.bigelow chemists.com - 7.30am-9pm, Sat 8.30am-7pm, Sun 8.30am-5.30pm.* This is the oldest pharmacy in the United States, dating from 1838. In completely retro environs, you'll find the best international cosmetic lines, as well as the C.O. Bigelow traditional apothecary products in their snazzy packaging: rose balm, cream with lemon extract, mint soap and essential oils.

⑪ Urban Outfitters – *B6* - *Corner of 14th St. & 6th Ave.* - Ⓜ *6th Ave.* - ℘ *646 638 1646 - www.urban outfitters.com - 10am-10pm, Sun 11am-10pm.* The store, set over two levels, is a favorite with aspiring hipsters and also sells streetwear and fashionable home goods. Multiple locations.

⑫ Uncle Sam's Army Navy Outfitters – *B6* - *37 West 8th St.* - *5th & 6th Ave* - Ⓜ *Washington Sq.* - ℘ *212 674 2222 - www.armynavy deals.com - 10am-8pm, Fri-Sat 10am-9pm, Sun 11am-7pm.* Outdoor goods surplus store; you'll find all-weather gear, hiking socks, and saddlebags.

㊱ Murray's – *B6* - *254 Bleecker St. - between 6th and 7th Ave* - Ⓜ *Christopher St.* - ℘ *212 243*

3289 - www.murrayscheese.com - Mon-Sat 8am-9pm, Sun 9am-6pm. A cheese-lover's paradise. There are no less than 350 kinds of cheese from Europe and the United States. You can eat at the cheese bar here or get tasty, ample sandwiches to go.

EAST VILLAGE

Area map p. 36

㊲ John Varvatos – *C7* - *315 Bowery - opposite Bleecker St.* Ⓜ *Astor Pl.* - ℘ *212 358 0315 - www.johnvarvatos.com - 12pm-8pm, Sat 11am-8pm, Sun 12pm-6pm.* An (expensive) fashion boutique in what was CBGB, a legendary rock club where Blondie and the Ramones started out. Some cry sacrilege, while others make rock pilgrimages here: the designer has aimed to preserve the spirit of the site, with the original walls and stage kept intact.

CHELSEA - MEATPACKING

⑰ OMG – *B5* - *217 7th Ave. - 22nd and 23rd Sts* - Ⓜ *23rd St.* - ℘ *212 807 8650 - www.omgjeans.com - 9.30am-9pm, Sun 10am-8pm.* A branch of a chain of denim shops that sell classic brands (Levi's, Lee, Pepe Jeans, Calvin Klein and Ralph Lauren) at cut prices. There are good bargains to be had.

⑱ Angel Thrift Shop – *B6* - *118 West 17th St. - between 6th and 7th Aves* - Ⓜ *18th St.* - ℘ *212 229 0546 - angelstreetthrift.org - 11am-7pm, Sat 10am-7pm, Sun 12pm-5pm.* The proceeds of this second-hand store

Shop window, Lexington Avenue

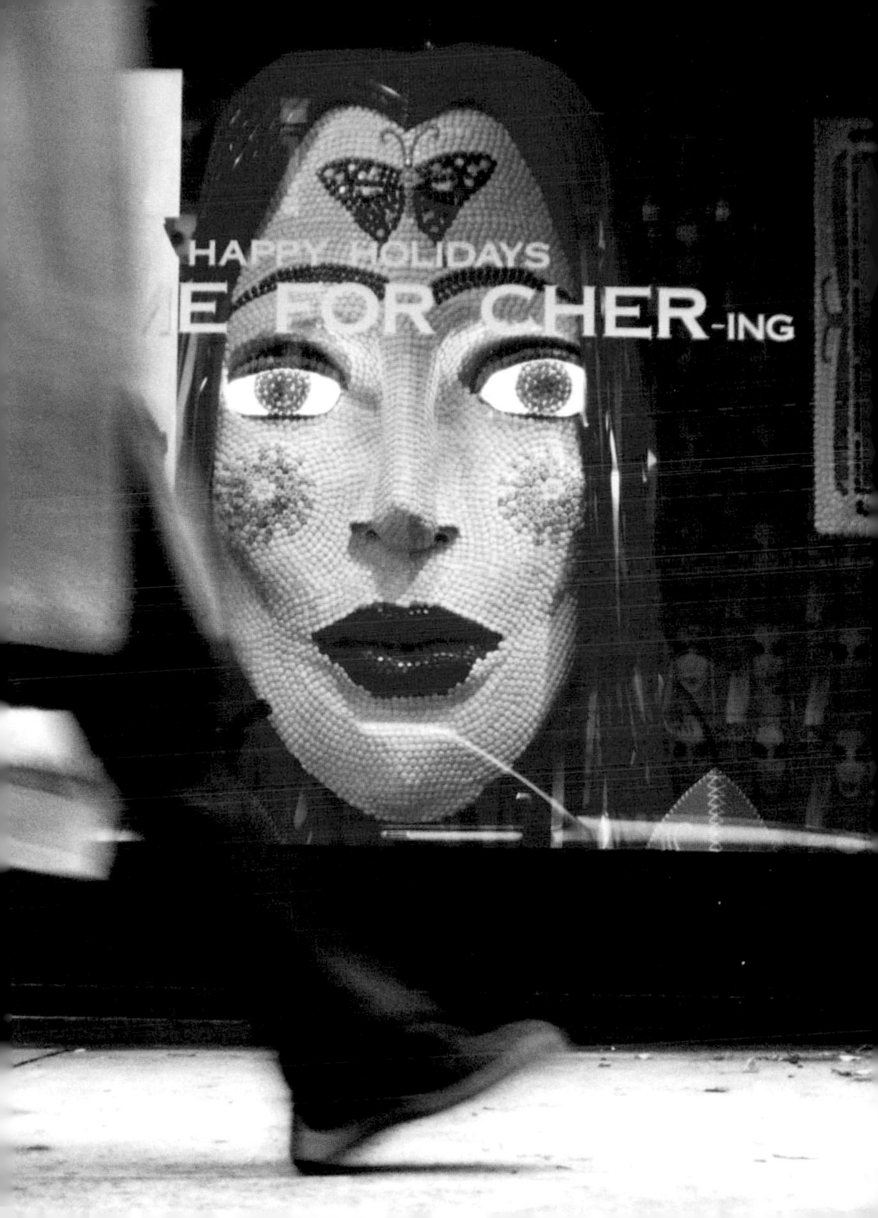
HAPPY HOLIDAYS
E FOR CHER-ING

go to charities helping drug addicts, HIV-positive people and those with mental health problems. Brands and individuals donate clothing, furniture and accessories. Some beautiful pieces at unbeatable prices.

34 Anthropologie – *B6* - *75 9th Ave. - Chelsea Market -* Ⓜ *23rd St. -* ℘ *212 620 3116 - www.anthropologie.com - 10am-9pm, Sun 10am-8pm - closed 25 Dec.* Inside Chelsea Market is an outpost of this bobo chain, and it makes shrewd use of the industrial architecture of the site. You'll find exclusive bohemian-style clothing, accessories and homewares in a simple, timeless style. Also sells beauty products and shoes.

122

Macy's, Sixth Avenue

© Anton J Geisser/age fotostock

UNION SQUARE

19 Strand – *C6* - *828 Broadway - corner of 12th St.-* Ⓜ *14th St./Union Sq. -* ℘ *212 473 1452 - www.strandbooks. com - 9.30am-10.30pm, Sun 11am-10.30pm.* A bookshop set across three levels offering cut prices; you'll find well-thumbed art books, foreign literature and all other kinds of assorted books, as well as a rare books section.

MIDTOWN WEST

21 Macy's – *C5* - *151 West 34th St. - Herald Sq. -* Ⓜ *34th St./Herald Sq. -* ℘ *212 695 4400 - www.macys.com - 10am-10pm, Wed 10am-11pm - closed Sun.* Practically anything you might want to buy can be found at Macy's, from big designer brands to dog collars. Between floors 8 and 9 is an original wooden escalator. ♿ *p. 54.*

22 B & H – *B5* - *420 9th Ave. - near 34th St. -* Ⓜ *34th St./Penn Sta. -* ℘ *212 444 6615 - www.bhphotovideo.com - 9am-6pm, Fri 9am-2pm, Sun 10am-5pm - closed Sat and certain public holidays (Christian and Jewish).* An address for image professionals. A vast choice of photo and video materials. Smart prices on refurbished goods.

23 NBA Store – *C5* - *545 5th Ave. -* Ⓜ *5th Ave. -* ℘ *212 457 3120 - www. nbanyc.fanatics.com - 9am-9pm, Sun 10am-7pm.* Team kit, accessories and gadgets for basketball fans.

MIDTOWN EAST

24 Saks Fifth Avenue – *C5* - *611 5th Ave. - 49th and 50th Sts* - Ⓜ *5th Ave. - ☎ 212 753 4000 - www.saksfifth avenue.com - 10am-8.30pm, Sun 11am-7pm - closed at Easter, Thanksgiving and Dec 25.* A legendary name, opened in 1924. Here you'll find all the upscale designers and big brands, set over ten floors.

25 Brooks Brothers – *C5* - *346 Madison Ave. - angle 44th St. -* Ⓜ *5th Ave. - ☎ 212 682 8800 - www. brooksbrothers.com - 8am-8pm, Sat 9am-7pm, Sun 11am-7pm - closed Thanksgiving & 25 Dec.* This chic tailor dressed the actors of the 1950s and dresses businesswomen and men today. You'll find made-to-measure or partially made-to-measure suits, ties and more.

26 Niketown – *D4* - *6 East 57th St. -* Ⓜ *5th Ave. - ☎ 212 891 6453 - www. nike.com - &. - 10am-8pm, Sun 11am-8pm - closed Thanksgiving & 25 Dec.* An ultra modern space with all the latest gear from the purveyors for the swoosh set.

UPPER EAST SIDE

28 Barneys – *D4* - *660 Madison Ave. - angle 61st St. -* Ⓜ *5th Ave./59th St. - ☎ 212 826 8900 - www.barneys.com - 10am-8pm, Sat 10am-7pm, Sun 11am-7pm - closed Thanksgiving & 25 Dec.* The trendiest of the department stores particularly promotes young designers. Expensive, but occasional sales.

29 Bloomingdale's – *D4* - *1000 3rd Ave. and 59th St (you can enter on Lexington Ave.) -* Ⓜ *59th St. - ☎ 212 7052 000 - www. bloomingdales.com - 10am-8.30pm, Sun 11am-7pm - closed Easter Sunday.* This is one of the most popular department stores because you can find just about everything there.

BROOKLYN - WILLIAMSBURG

37 Beacon's Closet – *F8* - *23 Bogart St. - 11237 Brooklyn - Bushwick -* Ⓜ *Morgan Ave. - ☎ 718 417 5683 - beaconscloset.com - 11am-8pm - closed 1st Jan, 4 Jul, Thanksgiving and 25 Dec.* In this giant thrift store you'll unearth vintage treasures for a handful of dollars. Another store in Park Slope at 92 5th Ave.

38 Space Ninety 8 – *E7* - *98 North 6th St. -* Ⓜ *Bedford Ave. - ☎ 718 599 0209 - www.uospaces.com/ninety8/ en/williamsburg-ny - 11am-9pm, Sun 11am-8pm.* The concept store of the brand Urban Outfitters is housed in former iron-framed warehouse, with brick walls reminiscent of Soho. Set over several levels, the vinyls, pop objects and printed tees reflect the spirit of Williamsburg. The restaurant, by Israeli-American *MasterChef* winner Ilan Hall, enjoys a strong reputation. There is also a popular rooftop.

31 Mast Brothers Chocolate – *D7* - *111 North 3rd St. -* Ⓜ *Bedford Ave. - ☎ 718 388 2625 - mastbrothers.com - 9am-8pm.* This is good chocolate but certainly not the best. However, the packaging makes these bars good gifts. Have a hot chocolate here and watch the bars being made.

Nightlife

As a general rule, **Downtown** (to the south of 30th St.) is the most lively part of Manhattan in the evenings: there is amusement for every taste. Midtown West, with **Broadway** and **Times Square**, is the theater district. The **Upper West Side** is still the place for quality concert halls, including Lincoln Center. To the north, **Harlem** is the home of jazz and blues. **27th and 28th Streets** (between 10th and 11th Avenues) is the go-to clubs that open, change name and go out of fashion at a head-spinning speed. Be warned that the drink prices are in line with the area's reputation aka they're steep.

If you want an unforgettable experience, go to **Harlem** for a gospel mass (Sunday 9am to 11pm). They last 1hr, with a mix of sermons and song (plan to bring change for the collection).

In **Brooklyn,** the bars and clubs of **Williamsburg, Greenpoint, and Bushwick** are hot and trending.

Magazines (online) *New York Magazine, Time Out New York, The New Yorker,* and *The Village Voice* (free) list concerts, shows and films.

Online box office – www.gotickets.com.

Kiosques TKTS – *Times Square (West 47th St. Enter at Broadway and 7th Ave.) and South St. Seaport (corner of Front and John Sts) - matinée performances 10am-2pm (11am-3pm Sun), evening show 3pm-8pm (7pm Sun) - arrive at least 30min before start time.* Tickets sold at 25 to 50% discount for shows next day or same day. Payment by cash or card.

♿ *Find the addresses on our maps using the numbers on the listings (ex. ❶). The coordinates in red (ex. C2) refer to the detachable map (inside the cover)*.

SOHO

Area map p. 31

❶ **SOB's (Sound of Brazil)** – *B6* - *204 Varick St. - near Houston St. -* Ⓜ *Houston St. - ✆ 212 243 4940 - sobs.com - ♿ - staring from 7pm.* Warm atmosphere and soft lighting. nightly concerts, salsa, samba, reggae and hip-hop. Friday, enjoy salsa classes; Saturdays are "Caribbean Saturdays" with DJs.

LOWER EAST SIDE

Area map p. 36

❷ **The Box** – *C7* - *189 Chrystie St. -* Ⓜ *Grand St., Bowery - ✆ 212 982 9301 - www.theboxnyc.com - from 11pm - closed Sun and Mon.* This café-theater aims to recreate the atmosphere of an old-school cabaret; expect burlesque numbers, contortionists, puppets and tap dancers. Entertainment guaranteed!

❸ **Bowery Ballroom** – *B7* - *6 Delancey St. -* Ⓜ *Bowery - ✆ 212 533 2111 - www.boweryballroom.com* A concert hall, one of the best in New York, and a bar, where famous rock groups play as well talented newcomers. Great acoustics.

GREENWICH VILLAGE

Area map p. 41

④ 55 Bar – *B6* - *55 Christopher St. - près de 7ᵗʰ Ave. -* Ⓜ *Christopher St. - ℘ 212 929 9883 - www.55bar.com - 2pm-4am.* In a little room dating from the Prohibition period, expect nightly quality jazz and blues concerts.

⑤ Village Underground – *B6* - *130 West 3ʳᵈ St. - near 6ᵗʰ Ave. -* Ⓜ *West 4ᵗʰ St. - ℘ 212 777 7745 - thevillageunderground.com - 9.30pm-3.30am, Sat 9pm-4am, Sun 9.30pm-3am.* This is a legendary space from the Sixties and Seventies when Bob Dylan, Joan Baez and Simon & Garfunkel played here. Intimate club known for its eclectic programming.

㉒ Café Wha? – *B6* - *115 Macdougal St. -* Ⓜ *9ᵗʰ St. - ℘ 212 254 3706 - cafewha.com - 8pm-3am.* One of the most famous live music venues in the city. Opened in the 1950s, this is where luminaries such as Bob Dylan started (with his first fee said to be \$16), as well as Jimi Hendrix, Janis Joplin and many others. The poets of the Beat Generation, including Ginsberg, recited poems here and some of the greatest American comedians have performed here. A performance at the legendary Café Wha? is still an obligatory rite of passage for rising stars today.

EAST VILLAGE

⑧ Joe's Pub – *C6* - *425 Lafayette St. - between East 4ᵗʰ St. and Astor Pl. -* Ⓜ *Astor Pl. - ℘ 212 539 8778 - www.joespub.com - from 7pm.* An intimate venue where you can drink and eat, with rich and varied programming. Alice Coltrane, Norah Jones, Hawksley Workman and Jamie Cullum have all played here.

CHELSEA - MEATPACKING

Area map p. 41

⑨ Highline Ballroom – *B6* - *431 West 16ᵗʰ St. between 9ᵗʰ and 10ᵗʰ Aves -* Ⓜ *23ʳᵈ St. - ℘ 212 414 5994 - highlineballroom.com -* & *- from 6pm or 7pm, 8pm or 11pm depending on the show, Sunday from 12.30pm to 2pm for brunch - opening hours vary.* A beautiful space with a dance floor and well-researched programming, from hip hop to electro: Rahzel, Ellen Allien, Mos Def, Lou Reed and Hot Chip have all passed through here.

⑱ Cielo – *B6* - *18 Little West 12ᵗʰ St. - between 9ᵗʰ Ave. and Washington St. -* Ⓜ *8ᵗʰ Ave. - ℘ 646 543 8556 - www.cieloclub.com.* Expect luxe design and high-quality programming (with a deep house slant) in this popular but intimate club.

MIDTOWN WEST

⑩ B.B. King Blues Club – *C5* - *237 West 42ⁿᵈ St. - 7ᵗʰ and 8ᵗʰ Sts -* Ⓜ *Times Square/42ⁿᵈ St. 7ᵗʰ and 8ᵗʰ Sts -* Ⓜ *Times Square/42ⁿᵈ St. - ℘ 212 997 4144 - www.bbkingblues.com -* 🅿 *\$25 -* & *- 11am-1am.* This is one of the best-known clubs on 42ⁿᵈ St. Expect top-quality concerts; "Beatles brunch" on Saturday and "Gospel Brunch" on Sunday.

125

UPPER WEST SIDE

⓫ The West End Lounge – *D2* - *955 West End Ave. - angle 107th St. -* Ⓜ *Cathedral Parkway 110th St. - ☎ 212 531 4759 - thewestendlounge.com - 4pm-4am, Sun 12pm-4am.* Excellent jazz, blues and rock club.

HARLEM

⓬ Apollo Theater – *E1* - *253 West 125th St. -* Ⓜ *125th St. - ☎ 212 531 5300 - www.apollotheater.org - opening hours vary depending on shows.* This is *the* legendary venue for jazz, R&B and soul. The famous Wednesday concerts *(Amateur Night, from 7.30pm)* are the place to catch the next big thing. ♿ *Harlem, p. 91.*

⓭ Canaan Baptist Church – *E2* - *132 West 116th St. - near Adam Clayton Blvd -* Ⓜ *116th St. - ☎ 212 866 0301 - www.cbccnyc.org - Sunday from 10am.* **First Corinthian Baptist Church – *E2* -** *1912 Adam Clayton Blvd (corner of 116th St.)* Ⓜ *116th St - www. fcbnyc.org.* Two churches where you can attend a gospel mass on Sunday morning. Spaces limited, arrive early.

BROOKLYN - WILLIAMSBURG

⓮ The Knitting Factory – *E7* - *361 Metropolitan Ave. - 11211 Brooklyn -* Ⓜ *Bedford Ave. - ☎ 347 529 6696 - www.knittingfactory.com - 6pm-3am, Sun 12pm-3.30am.* Bar and eclectic live music, from acid jazz to rock and electro.

⓯ Brooklyn Bowl – *E7* - *61 Wythe Ave. - 11249 Brooklyn -* Ⓜ *Nassau Ave. - ☎ 718 963 3369 - www.brooklyn bowl.com - ♿ - from 6pm, Sat-Sun from 11am.* As well as being a pricey bowling alley *($25/30min, shoe rental $5)*, this club hosts themed parties, karaoke, DJs and rock concerts. An eclectic venue offering an original experience.

⓰ Union Pool – *E7* - *484 Union Ave. - 11211 Brooklyn -* Ⓜ *Lorimer St.- ☎ 718 609 0484 - www.union-pool.com - 5pm-4am, Sat-Sun 2pm-4am.* Both a bar and a live music venue, this Williamsburg staple never goes out of fashion. The large garden decorated with strings of lanterns is another draw; here, you can refuel from El Diablo Tacos food truck.

😊 ⓱ Output – *E7* - *74 Wythe Ave. - 11249 Brooklyn -* Ⓜ *Nassau Ave. - outputclub.com.* Created in the model of a Berlin club, Output is considered one of the best on the East Coast, thanks to on-point programming (house), powerful (but not oppressive) sound and impressive light shows. In warm weather, DJ-cocktail sessions on Sunday afternoons on the roof are super popular. Enjoy a magnificent view over Manhattan *(no entry fee).*

Where to stay

This is where the biggest part of your budget will be spent. Don't forget to add taxes (14.25 %) and tips (🕯 *p. 137*).

You can reserve flight+ hotel packages through low-cost tour operators (🕯 *p. 134*) or go through **booking centers**: www.hotel-discount.com, www.nyc.com. **Hotels** and **Bed & Breakfasts** (www.bbonline.com, www.bedandbreakfast.com) have equivalent rates. If you like going out, go for areas located between Canal and 30th Sts. If you plan to spend much time in Times Square, try Midtown West. Lower Manhattan (Financial District) empties in the evening and is thus fairly quiet. Practically all the hotels listed here have **free WiFi**.

🕯 *Find the addresses on the detachable map (inside the cover) using the numbers in the listing (ex. 1). The coordinates in red (ex. D2) refer to the same map.*

LOWER MANHATTAN

From $240 to $360

24 World Center Hotel – *A8* - 144 Washington St. - Ⓜ Cortland St. - ✆ 212 577 2933 - www.worldcenter hotel.com - 🖥 ✕ - 🅿 pay - 169 rooms $189/$329. Built opposite the World Trade Center. Spectacular views over the site and the skyscrapers of Lower Manhattan, especially from the terrace on the 20th floor. Design

is well thought-out in the rooms and they are kitted out with good tech.

CHINATOWN - LITTLE ITALY

From $240 to $360

12 Best Western Bowery Hanbee – *B7* - 231 Grand St. - Ⓜ Grand St. - ✆ 212 925 1177 - www.bw-bowery hanbeehotel.com - 🖥 - 99 rooms $219/299 🖵. At the meeting point of Chinatown and Little Italy, this pristine new hotel offers good value for money; small but bright and well put-together rooms.

SOHO

From $240 to $360

17 Hotel Hugo – *A7* - 525 Greenwich St. - Ⓜ Spring St. - ✆ 212 608 4848 - hotelhugony.com - 🖥 - 122 rooms $240/ $350. Tucked away in a quiet corner of Soho, the lobby and rooms of this attractive and discreet hotel are evocative of a luxury ocean liner: think lacquered wood paneling, clean lines, and elegant décor in darker tones. Superb rooftop, (🕯 *Azul On The Rooftop, p. 114*).

More than $ 600

8 The Mercer – *B7* - 147 Mercer St. - angle Prince St. - Ⓜ Prince St. - ✆ 212 966 6060 - www.mercer hotel.com - 🖥 ✕ - 🅿 pay - ♿ - 75 rooms. $446/ $650. Artfully decorated mini-lofts, courtesy of

French designer Christian Liaigre. Impeccable service. An excellent address with a price to match.

LOWER EAST SIDE

From $ 220 to 250

13 **East Houston Hotel** – **C7** - *151 East Houston St. -* Ⓜ *Lower East Side/2ⁿᵈ Ave. -* ☏ *212 777 0012 - www.hoteleasthouston.com -* 🖥 *-* 🅿 *pay -* ♿ *- 42 rooms $182/279* 🛏 On a busy avenue but super central, this is a modern hotel with slightly cramped but well-appointed rooms in a great location.

More than $250

9 **Off Soho Suites Hotel** – **B7** - *11 Rivington St. -* Ⓜ *Bowery -* ☏ *212 979 9815 www.offsoho.com -* 🖥 ♿ *- 38studios and apartments. (2 to 4 people) $249/500 (depending on occupation rate).* The name fits—the hotel is in LES but just off Soho — and it offers the economical option to stay in an apartment with a kitchen Second branch to the north of the East Village.

GREENWICH VILLAGE

From $220 to $250

1 **Larchmont Hotel** – **B6** - *27 West 11ᵗʰ St. -* Ⓜ *14ᵗʰ St./Union Sq. -* ☏ *212 989 9333 -* 🖥 *- 55 rooms $189/249* 🛏*.* A quiet tree-lined road houses this very pleasant and clean hotel. Rooms decorated in soft tones; they're not huge but are all equipped with a washbasin. Communal bathrooms. Light breakfast.

14 **Washington Square Hotel** – **B6** - *103 Waverly Pl. -* Ⓜ *4ᵗʰ St./Washington Square -* ☏ *212 777 9515 - www.washingtonsquarehotel.com -* 🖥 *-* 🅿 *pay - 149 rooms $ 220/ $ 282 -* 🍴 *dishes $23/$34.* Familial hotel in Art Deco style, inspired by cinema photography. Rooms are modestly sized but very light. Attentive service.

EAST VILLAGE

Less than $200

15 **St. Mark's Hotel** – **C6** - *2 St Mark's Pl. -* Ⓜ *Astor Pl. -* ☏ *212 674 0100 - www.stmarkshotel.net -* 🖥 *- 64 rooms $ 120/140.* The comforts are basic, there are single beds and it's quite noisy, but it is well maintained. Ideally located for heavy sleepers who like going out at night. No elevator.

More than $300

2 **The Bowery Hotel** – **C7** - *335 Bowery -* Ⓜ *Bleecker St. -* ☏ *212 505 9100 - www.theboweryhotel.com -* 🖥 🍴 *-* 🅿 *pay -* ♿ *- 135 rooms. $365/$455.* The charm of Old Europe is in evidence in this establishment. Some rooms have a private terrace with a view over the city. Very good Italian food in the hotel restaurant.

CHELSEA - MEATPACKING

From $145 to $375

16 **Chelsea Savoy** – **B5** - *204 West 23ʳᵈ St. -* Ⓜ *23ʳᵈ St. -* ☏ *212 929 9353 - www.chelseasavoy.com -* 🖥 ♿ *- 98 rooms $145/375.* Located near public transportation, this is a comfortable hotel; it is quite impersonal but well-equipped. The rooms on the first floor street side can be noisy.

😊 27 **Fairfield Inn & Suites New York** – *C5* - *116 West 28th St. - on the corner of Ave. of the Americas -* Ⓜ *28th St. - ☎ 212 206 0998 - fairfield. marriott.com -* 🖃 *-* 🅿 *$39/$49 -* 🚹 *- 110 rooms $299/$559* 🛏. An excellent hotel, which is particularly well situated. It's hard to fault. The welcome is warm and efficient, the rooms are decently sized, clean and demurely (but elegantly) decorated, with wood furnishings. The breakfast is generous. Recommended.

MADISON SQUARE

From $160 to $300

18 **Clarion Hotel Park Avenue** – *C5* - *429 Park Ave. South -* Ⓜ *28th St. - ☎ 212 532 4860 - www.clarionpark.com -* 🖃 *-* 🅿 *Pay- 60 rooms $209/$259.* Though they are a little impersonal, the rooms are light and pleasant. Those facing the back of the hotel are quieter but a bit dark.

4 **The Evelyn** – *C5* - *7 East 27th St. - between Madison and 5th Aves. -* Ⓜ *28th St. - ☎ 212 545 8000 - www. theevelyn.com -* ✕ *-* 🅿 *Pay -* 🚹 *- wifi - 170 rooms $239/$289.* The flamboyantly decorated facade and colorful décor are the big draws of this hotel, which attracts young artists and fashion professionals.

MIDTOWN WEST

From $160 to $250

20 **The Hotel @ Times Square** – *C5* - *59 West 46th St. -* Ⓜ *Times Square - ☎ 212 790 2710 - www.applecore hotels.com -* 🖃 *-* 🅿 *$27/37/24h - 213 rooms $180/$220* 🛏. Steps from Times Square but not too noisy. Renovated in light and functional style. Well equipped rooms.

From $240 to $360

19 **414 Hotel** – *C4* - *414 West 46th St. - 9th and 10th Aves. -* Ⓜ *50th St. - ☎ 212 399 0006 - www.414hotel.com -* 🖃 ✕ *- 22 rooms $249/$309* 🛏. Set in the quiet of a tree-lined road, this hotel is housed across two brick houses joined by a pretty patio. The rooms are a little small and soberly decorated in a very New York style. The overall effect is a relaxing atmosphere with the feel of a family hotel.

10 **Room Mate Grace Hotel** – *C5* - *125 West 45th St. - 6th and 7th Aves -* Ⓜ *Times Square - ☎ 212 354 2323 - www.room-matehotels.com -* 🖃 🛏 *- 139 rooms $269/$339.* Right in the heart of Times Square, the little rooms here are designed like boat cabins, but the general look is modern, colorful and functional. Indoor pool (evenings only) and sauna. Trendy, thus the slightly over-inflated prices.

5 **Hudson Hotel** – *C4* - *358 West 58th St. -* Ⓜ *Columbus Circle - ☎ 212 554 6000 - www.hudsonhotel.com -* 🖃 ✕ 🚹 *- 866 rooms $224/$312.* The interiors of this former boarding school, renovated by Philippe Starck,

present a whirlwind of grandeur and eclecticism. Very pleasant terrace with a view over Central Park. The modest size of the rooms is compensated for by attractive deals on the hotel's website.

㉑ Belvedere – *C4* - *319 West 48th St. - Ⓜ 49th St. - ☎ 212 245 7000 - www. belvederehotelnyc.com - ▤ ✕ - ℗ pay - ♿ - 400 rooms. $229/$323.* A little removed from the activity of Times Square, a beautiful hotel in the great tradition of New York Art deco. Elegant and spacious rooms, which enjoy lots of natural light at the front of the hotel, equipped with all the best comforts. Impeccable service. Special promotions on website.

MIDTOWN EAST

From $160 to $250

㉒ Ramada Inn Eastside – *C5* - *161 Lexington Ave. - Ⓜ 33rd St. - ☎ 212 545 1800 - applecorehotels.com - ▤ - ℗ $30 - ♿ - 111 rooms. $148/$180 ☕.* In the southern part of Murray Hill, a very classic chain hotel, well served by public transport. Modern and comfortable rooms. Considerate service.

More than $250

⑪ W New York Hotel – *D5* - *541 Lexington Ave. - 49th and 50th Sts. - Ⓜ 51th St. and Lexington Ave. - ☎ 212 755 1200 - www.wnewyork.com - ▤ ✕ - ℗ $ 65/75/day - ♿ - 688 rooms. $233/ $280.* A few minutes by foot from the Chrysler Building, this hotel offers comfortably equipped rooms with chic and pared-down décor. Note: the least expensive rooms can be small and a little dark.

☺ ⑥ The Library – *C5* - *299 Madison Ave. - Ⓜ Grand Central - ☎ 212 983 4500 - www.library hotel.com - ▤ ♿ - 60 rooms $223/ $447 ☕.* Elegant, welcoming and quiet, and filled with books (more than 6 000!). Design décor and superb terrace.

UPPER WEST SIDE

More than $250

㉓ Belleclaire Hotel – *C3* - *250 West 77th St. - Ⓜ 79th St. - ☎ 212 362 7700 - www.hotelbelleclaire.com - ▤ - ℗ $51/24hr - ♿ - 244 rooms $229/$459.* Close to Central Park and the Lincoln Center, in a quiet residential neighborhood. Expect simple, well-maintained rooms with understated décor, all equipped with a refrigerator. Good value for money.

UPPER EAST SIDE

From $375

☺ ㉕ Loews Regency – *D4* - *540 Park Ave. - Ⓜ Lexington Ave. - ☎ 212 759 4100 - www.loewshotels.com - ▤ ✕ - ℗ $80/24h - ♿ - 379 rooms and 58 suites $359/$1 169 ☕.* Light and spacious rooms decorated simply mixing light colors and contemporary touches. Friendly and effective service. One of the best in its category, close to Central Park, the Met and the subway.

131

Planning Your Trip

Williamsburg Bridge and Downtown Manhattan
© T. Shi Photography/Moment/Getty Images

Know before you go

ENTRY REQUIREMENTS

ID – To enter the United States without a visa, you will need a **biometric** passport issued after 26 October **2006**. In all other cases, obtaining a visa is obligatory. If in doubt, consult the webiste of the American Embassy.

Visa – If you have a valid passport and are travelling for business or leisure for **less than three months**, a visa is not necessary. If your trip does not fit this criteria, a visa is obligatory and if it is likely you will exercise a professional activity during your stay.

ESTA (Electronic System for Travel Authorization) – Since January 2009, it has been obligatory for travellers without visas to fill in, at least 72 hours before departure, an **electronic questionnaire** (health, criminal record, etc.) available on embassy website.

Customs– Arms, drugs, vegetable products and food products and some kinds of medications are forbidden on American soil. The following are permitted: 1 l of alcohol (for over 21s), 200 cigarettes, 50 cigars or 2 kg of tobacco. Gifts must represent a sum of less than $100 (keep your receipts).

Other elements to provide – A **return ticket**, plane or boat, and the **address** of where you're staying. Without these you risk being turned back. Electronic devices must not be out of battery.

GETTING TO NEW YORK

♿ To find out more about **airports**, go to *Getting to New York, p. 3*.

The main providers

Air France – ☎ 36 54 (€ 0.35/min) - www.airfrance.fr.
American Airlines – ☎ 0 821 980 999 (€ 0.12/min) - www.americanairlines.fr.
Delta Airlines – ☎ 0892 702 609 - www.delta.com.
Icelandair – ☎ 01 44 51 60 51 - www.icelandair.fr.
KLM – ☎ 09 69 36 86 05 (reservations) - www.klm.com.

Low-cost agencies

Travel agents compare prices and offer flight bookings or package deals. Here is a selection:
E-Dreams – www.edreams.fr
Easy Vols – www.easyvols.fr
Expedia – www.expedia.fr

MONEY

The **dollar** ($) is divided into 100 **cents**. You'll find bills of 1, 5, 10, 50 and 100 dollars, and coins of 1, 5, 10, 25 and 50 cents. A dime is worth 10 cents, a quarter 25 cents.
Exchange rate: around $1 for £0.71 (March 2018).
Credit cards – Accepted, without a limit for payments. The exchange rate is made on the day of the transaction, with a commission added.
Cash points /ATMs – Available

throughout the city, they apply the exchange rate at the time of the transaction, and a flat commission is taken. It is better value to take out a large sum.

HEALTH INSURANCE

Do not scrimp on health insurance, as fees can rise very high and very quickly indeed. Tour operators generally propose a very comprehensive insurance policy. Check with your bank whether international coverage is included with your bank card. Work out exactly what the steps to follow are in the case of an accident, and which forms you need to fill out.

SEASONS

New York has a temperate continental climate, which is fairly humid and characterised with a wide temperature range.
Summer – The average temperature hovers at around 30 °C in the day, and a little below 20 °C at night
Winter – Cold and humid with some fine sunny days. In December to February, temperatures can fall to under 0 °C? The winter is only really harsh when there are blizzards, accompanied by snow. Celebrate Christmas and New Year at Times Square.
Spring and autumn – Mild, between 15 and 25 °C. The transition of May-June is one of the most pleasant times of year. The autumn, in the glow of Indian summer, is the start of the cultural season, a time for shopping

and for celebrations (Halloween, Thanksgiving).
Precipitation – Throughout the year; bring an umbrella.

INFORMATION

Websites
City of New York – www.nyc.gov
Restaurants, cultural agendas – www.timeoutny.com
http://nymag.com
www.nytimes.com
www.villagevoice.com

Tourist offices
Tourist office – www.nycgo.com
In the city there are several branches of the **Official NYC Information Center** :
Midtown – 151 W 34th St. - Mon-Fri 9am-7pm, Sat 10am-7pm, Sun 11am-7pm.
Times Square Broadway Plaza – between 43rd and 44th St. - www.timessquarenyc.org - daily 9am-8pm.
City Hall – South tip of City Hall Park (on Broadway level with Park Row) - Mon-Fri 9am-6pm, w/e 10am-5pm, public holidays 9am-3pm.
South Street Seaport – On the banks of the East River - Pier 15, in line with Hornblower Cruises - May-Aug : daily 9am-7pm; Sep-April: daily 9am-5pm.

Two other info points:
Lower East Side Visitor Center – 54 Orchard St. - Mon-Fri 10am-6pm, w/e 12pm-5pm.
Official NYC Information Kiosk (Chinatown) – At the intersection of Canal St., Walker St. and Baxter St. - daily 10am-6pm, public holidays, 10am-3pm.

Basic information

BANKS

There are banks and ATMs on practically every corner. Unless you use your own bank, expect to pay a fee of $2.50-4. ♿ *Money, p. 134 and Opening hours, facing page.*

BIKES

Traffic in New York can be crazy. Unless you have experience with urban cycling, you should cycle only in parks and protected bike lanes. There are many shops that rent bikes. New York's bike share program is called **Citi Bike**, and there are docks everywhere. $12/24 hours (unlimited 30min rides). **www.citibikenyc.com**.

BOATS

Ferry

East River The ferry plies the East River, stopping in Manhattan, Brooklyn, Queens, and Governor's Island (seasonal). $2.75/single ride (free transfer available). Expect lines. *www.ferry.nyc*

IKEA – IKEA run a ferry between Pier 11/Wall St. and Red Hook. $5 on weekdays (but free with purchase of at least $10). Free on weekends. Free for under 12. Expect lines.

Hop-on/Hop-off $35, valid for a day for unlimited journeys. ℘ 212 445-7599 - www.citysightseeingnewyork.com

Staten Island - The ferry (free, 24hr/day) leaves from South Ferry in Battery Park (♿ *p. 25*). Good view of Statue of Liberty.

CONSULATES

Consulate of Canada – 1251 6th Ave b/t 49th and 50th Sts. - ℘ 212 596-1628 - international.gc.ca/ - Mon-Fri 9am-12pm, 1-3pm.

British Consulate – 845 3rd Ave., - ℘ 212 745 0200 - www.gov.uk - Mon-Fri 9am-4pm (by appointment only unless emergency).

Australian Consulate – 150 E 42nd St - ℘ 212 351 6500- newyork.consulate.gov.au - Mon-Fri 9am-5pm.

IKEA shuttle

© Y. Kanazawa/Michelin

EATING OUT

You can eat at all hours in New York: the local routine is a hearty breakfast from 7am, a light lunch on the go, with dinner remaining the most important meal of the day (until 11pm). On weekends, **brunch** serves as breakfast and lunch (between 10am and 4pm). Options in New York include street stands and food trucks (under $8) food from around the world (less than $12 in small shops), and restaurants for varying budgets. There are special deals (*Early Bird* or the *Pre-Theater Menu*) served in the early evening, between 5pm and 7pm or 7.30pm : with these, you can get dinner for less than $30. **Drinks** at restaurants are expensive, particularly wine, which is served by the glass ($8 to $15). Some restaurants are BYOB. Tax (8.875 %) and tip (15-20%) are not included in listed prices

Many **grocery stores** have a prepared foods section, offering salads and hot dishes. ☙ *Tips p. 141 and Addresses/Where to eat, p. 104.*

ELECTRICITY

American plug sockets are different to British plugs. Bring an adapter from home. The current here is 110V.

INTERNET

Many cafés, some bars and most hotels offer free WiFi. There is also the possibility of network access in public parks. LinkNYC kiosks on the street provide free WiFi and charging ports.

Emergencies
Emergency services: ✆ *911 for police, fire, medical.*

OPENING HOURS

Shops – Mon-Sat 10am-7 or 8pm. Many shops do stay open until 9 or 10pm. Everything is open Sundays but usually at 11am. Many convenience stores and pharmacies are open 24/7.

Banks – Mon-Fri 9am-3.30pm, sometimes Sat 9am-12pm.

Pharmacies – Duane Reade, Walgreens, and CVS are everywhere, and many are open 24/7.

Post Office – Mon-Fri 8.30am-5pm or 6pm, Sat morning, opening hours vary. The Central Post Office (441, 8th Ave.) is open 24hr/day.

PRESS

Newspapers – *New York Times* (paper of record), *New York Post, New York Daily News* (tabloids).

Magazines – *Time Out New York* and *New York Magazine* are weekly magazines that cover cultural outings and the city's latest hot spots. *The New Yorker* is known for the quality of its writing and sophistication of its criticism.

POST

Price of a stamp: $ 1.15 for a postcard or letter (28g/1oz maximum). Allow a week for delivery to Europe.

PUBLIC HOLIDAYS

New Year's Day: Jan. 1

Martin Luther King Jr.'s Birthday: 3rd Monday of January.

Presidents Day: 3rd Monday of February.
Memorial Day: Last Monday of May.
Independence Day: July 4.
Labor Day: 1st Monday of September.
Columbus Day: 2nd Monday of October.
Veterans Day: November 11.
Thanksgiving Day: 4th Thursday of November.
Christmas Day: 25 December.

PUBLIC TRANSPORT

Public transport is the most economical and often fastest way to get around New York. The transport network—bus, subway and regional trains— is administered by the MTA (Metropolitan Transportation Authority): **www.mta.info**. Free maps in stations and online.
Subway map on the back of the detachable map.

Subway

Tickets and prices– A single ride ticket ($2.75) is valid for one journey including transfers to other subway lines but not to the bus.
The pay-per-ride **MetroCard** can be charged from $5.50 to $80. A new MetroCard itself costs $1. You can transfer between bus and subway once (within 2hrs of swiping). Refill the card as many times as you like (5% bonus each time you charge $5.50 or more. It can swiped a maximum of four times in a row.
Unlimited Ride MetroCard: 7-Day ($32) and 30-day ($121): unlimited access to metro and bus.
Getting around in the metro – Lines have a number or a letter. When identifying which platform to take, it's either the **direction** that counts (Downtown, Uptown) or the **destination** (Brooklyn, Queens, Manhattan). Look closely at the signs. In some stations, there is a separate entrance for each direction, and once you have passed through with your ticket, it will no longer be valid in the other direction if you make a mistake. Some lines are local, others express: an announcement will say what kind of train it is before the train arrives. Several lines, such as the C and E, 2 and 3, or 4 and 5, use the same platform, look closely at the **number** or **letter** displayed on the front of the train and on the side of the car. If you have an unlimited ride card and you exit the subway station, you'll have to wait 18min before you can use your card again.
Subways run **24hr/day**, every 2 to 5min at rush hour (7.30am-9am, 5pm-6.30pm) and up to 20min between 12am and 6.30am. A few stations are closed at night.
Safety – The subway is safe but, as with any big city, some care and caution is advised. Note that if a subway car is empty, there is a reason and it should be avoided.

Bus

The pricing system is the same as for the subway. MetroCards can

Subway trains in Queens

also be used on the buses. Lines are distinguished by a **number**. The preceding letter indicates the corresponding borough: M for Manhattan, B for Brooklyn, Bx for Bronx, Q for Queens. In Manhattan, the cross-town buses have the numbers of the streets on which they drive (ex. M34 = 34th St). To ask for the next stop (every two or three blocks), press the red "Stop" buttons or the vertical yellow strips between the windows. Many lines run **24hr/day** (less frequent at night). Between 8pm and 5am, you can ask the driver to let you off anywhere on the route.

Transfers – If you have a pay-per-ride MetroCard, changes from bus to metro or one bus to another are included in your ticket for 2 hours after first using it. If you have an Unlimited Ride MetroCard, changes are unlimited. If you are paying with cash, transfers are only free for bus lines that intersect with the one you have taken. To use cash, you need exact change in coins only (no bills). Ⓖ *Getting to New York p. 3.*

SIGHTSEEING

Most museums are closed Mondays and on the main public holidays. Tickets are expensive, but the museums have set times where entry is free.

Various **passes** offer entry to a selection of museums and tourist sites for a flat rate. Pamphlets are available in tourist offices, hotels and online. The **City Pass** offers the best deal. It is valid for nine days and costs $122 for an adult, $98 for a child aged between 6 and 17. It includes access to the Empire State Building, the Metropolitan Museum of Art and the American Museum of Natural History, as well as 3 other museums chosen from : the Guggenheim, Top of the Rock, the Statue of Liberty, the Circle Line cruise, 9/11 Memorial & Museum or Intrepid Sea, Air & Space Museum. See *www.citypass.com*.

The **New York Pass** exists in 1-day ($109), 2-day ($189), 3-day ($199) 5-day ($ 229) and 7-day ($289) versions. Cheaper online : www. newyorkpass.com. Calculate carefully what is viable, because it is impossible to see everything in the time given. It gives entry, among others, to a cruise around Manhattan, to the Empire State Building, the Museum of Natural History and many themed routes, guided tours and attractions, as well as the major museums (MoMA, Guggenheim, Met, Whitney, but not the Frick). Reductions in shops and restaurants, and for Broadway shows. It is particularly suited to families with children.

TAXES

Prices are always given without tax (including in this guide). Tax + tips inflate the bill by 25-30 %. In hotels, the tax is 14.25 %. For restaurants and all other products and services (décor, bike hire, etc.), it is 8.875 %. Clothing under $110 is not taxed. There is no tax on groceries, diapers, newspapers and magazines, laundry services, and a few other things.

TAXI

Initial charge – $2.50.

Meter – $0.40 per 0.2 miles, or $0.40/min stopped or significantly slowed down.

Rush hour – Mon-Fri 4pm-8pm, $1/journey supplement.

Night – 8pm-6am, supplement $0.50/journey.

City tax – $0.50/journey.

Tip – $1 (not obligatory but strongly recommended).

Maximum number of passengers: 4 unless in a van.

Taxis are available if their roof light (with number) is on.

The website **www.nyc.taxiwiz.com** gives you a price estimation for your journey. ☙ *Getting to New York, p. 3.*

CAR SERVICES

There are four main app-based car services in NYC: **Lyft**, **Juno**, **Via**, and **Uber**. Pricing is usually similar. These are almost always less expensive than a taxi, especially if you choose a shared ride instead of private. During rush hour, a taxi to the airport will usually cost less than a car service because it is a flat rate.

TIME DIFFERENCE

New York is on Eastern Standard Time (EST), **5hrs** behind London.
The change to **summer time** takes place in March to, and the change to **winter time** in November.

TELEPHONE

From overseas to New York

To call New York, dial 1, followed by the area code, and the 7 figures of the number of the person you're calling. For Manhattan, the area code is 212, 646 or 917. For the other boroughs (Brooklyn, Bronx, Queens and Staten Island), it's 718. Numbers preceded by 800 or 1-800 are *toll-free* inside the United States. It is now possible to use them from abroad by replacing them by 880 or 881.

From New York to overseas

To call Europe, dial 011 followed by the country code (UK 44), then the number of the person you're calling minus the first '0'.

From New York to New York

Dial the area code directly followed by the 7 figures of the number of the person you're calling. Information : 411 (free call in phone booths).
Mobile phones– Your phone must be 3G- or 4G-enabled to work. Before your trip, contact your provider to find out the rates for the US. You can buy an American SIM card at shops like T-Mobile, and also in most convenience stores and corner shops. These cards usually include a certain number of calls, SMS and data; sometimes calls and SMS are unlimited.

TIPS

Except when service is included (which is not very common), it is customary to leave between 15%

and 20% of the bill. In a hotel, $1 to a porter (for 1-2 bags), and *at least* $3 daily for housekeeping.

TOBACCO

Smoking is not allowed in public transport, offices, hotels, taxis, restaurants or bars. It is generally allowed only in some parks and on the street.
Cigarettes are expensive and can be bought in drug stores, corner stores and kiosks. Prices vary depending on the area.

TOILETS

There are not many public toilets *(rest rooms)*. You will find them in parks. Starbucks is popular for its toilets.

TOURS

There are a plethora of options on offer, consult: **www.nycgo.com**, which lists them.

By foot

Big Apple Greeter – www.bigapple greeter.org. To discover the city from inside with volunteering New-Yorkers (get in touch 2-3 weeks before). Free, but tips welcome.

Greenwich Village Literary Pub Crawl – ☏ 917 865 4575 - http://literarypubcrawl.com - Fri-Sun. meeting at 1pm at White Horse Tavern, 567 Hudson St. - $30 (reductions $25). Head off on the trail of famous actors (Jack Kerouac) and abstract expressionist painters (Jackson Pollock), and drink in the bars that they frequented.

Joyce Gold – ☏ 212 242 5762 - http://joycegoldhistorytours.com - $20 per person. Historical routes; timetable on website.

Urban Oyster Tour – ☏ (347) 618 TOUR (8687) - www.urbanoyster.com - from $ 69 (tastings included) for tours of about 3hrs. Interesting themed visits around food and drink.

Bus, boat, helicopter

Circle Line Cruises – ☏ 212 563 3200 - www.circleline42.com. Mini-cruises around Manhattan on river boat, The Beast for 30min ($29, 3-12 years $ 24) or you can take it a little slower, with a 2hr30min ride ($42, 3-12 years $35).

Gray Line – 777 8th Ave. (between 47th and 48th Sts) - ☏ 800 669 0051 or 212 445 0848 - www.newyork sightseeing.com - embankments 7am-8pm. The most complete offer for visiting New York on a double-decker bus (from $49). Reductions if you buy your tickets online.

On Location Tours – ☏ 212 683 2027 - onlocationtours.com - from $25 to $52. TV fans will love these bus journeys around the filming locations and memorable sites from the series.

Liberty Helicopters – ☏ 800 542 9933 - www.libertyhelicopters.com - from $ 214 (around 15min flight time). Fly over New York in a helicopter; prices vary depending on the duration of the flight. Note that this company has had several fatal crashes.

Festivals and events

ANNUAL EVENTS

January
▶ **Winter Antiques Show** – Seventh Regiment Armory, Park Avenue - January 18-27 - winterantiquesshow.com.

February
▶**Empire State Building Run-Up** – Race up the stairs of the skyscraper -
▶**Chinese New Year Festival** – Chinatown (in either Jan or Feb, depends on lunar calendar)
▶**Black History Month** – Events around the theme of black identity.
▶**Westminster Dog Show** – Madison Square Garden - www.westminsterkennelclub.org.

March
▶**Armory Arts Week** – Large contemporary art fair at Pier 94 - www.armoryartsweek.com.
▶**St Patrick's Day** – parade on 5th Avenue - March 17.
▶**Macy's Spring Flower Show** – Thousands of flowers are displayed in the Macy's windows for two week in late March.
▶**New Directors/New Film** – Lincoln Center and MoMA, 10 days in late March to discover rising filmmakers from around the world
▶**Easter Sunday Parade** – Parade on 5th Avenue - Easter Sunday.

April
▶**Spring Flower Exhibition** – , New York Botanical Garden - from mid-April until June.
▶**Tribeca Film Festival** – Independent film festival (👌 *p. 32*) - late April - https://tribecafilm.com/festival.
▶**Central Brooklyn Jazz Festival** – Jazz concerts from mid-April to mid-May- www.centralbrooklynjazzconsortium.org.
▶**Art Expo New York** – Pier 94 on the Hudson River - mid-late April - www.artexponewyork.com.

May
▶**Cherry Blossom Festival** – At Brooklyn Botanic Garden - beginning of May.
▶**Five Boro Bike Tour** – 67km/41mi of bike route around the five boroughs - 1st Sunday of May - www.bike.nyc.
▶**Memorial Day Parades** – Parades in all areas in memory of military personnel who died in service - 4th Monday of May.
▶**Washington Square Outdoor Art Exhibit** – last wknd. of May/first wknd. of June at Washington Square. There is also a September edition - www.wsoae.org.

June
▶**Museum Mile Festival** – Festival of Upper East Side museums - 2nd Tues. of June - museummilefestival.org.
▶**Puerto Rican Day Parade** – on 5th Avenue - 2nd Sun of June.

144

▶**NY Philharmonic Parks Concerts** – Free concerts in different parks - mid-June - www.nycgovparks.org.

▶**Mermaid Parade** – At Coney Island - mid June, a colorful mermaid parade - www.coneyisland.com.

▶**Lesbian and Gay Pride Week** – Parade along 5th Avenue - end of June.

▶**SummerStage** – Various open-air shows and concerts, some free. Performances most nights. - June through August - www.cityparksfoundation.org.

▶**Midsummer Night's Swing** – Concerts and dance shows on the plaza of the Lincoln Center - June 26-July 14 - www.lincolncenter.org/midsummer-night-swing.

July - August

▶**Independence Day** – National Day: 4 July, fireworks on the Hudson and the East River and boat parade at South Street Seaport.

▶**Shakespeare in the Park** – Open-air in Central Park - July-August - www.centralpark.com.

▶**Mostly Mozart Festival** – Concerts at the Lincoln Center - July 20-August 25 - www.lincolncenter.org/mostly-mozart.

▶**Feast of O-Bon** – Buddhist and Japanese festival celebrating the souls of ancestors in Riverside Park - the Saturday closest to the full moon.

▶**Harlem Summer Stage** – Dance, music and a range of events - July-Aug - harlemlocal.com.

▶**Lincoln Center Out of Doors** – Free concerts and ballet held in the open air, over three days - end of July - http://lcoutofdoors.org.

▶**NYC Restaurant Week® Summer** – Modestly priced menus in well-reputed restaurants - end of July to mid-Aug - nycgo.com/restaurantweek.

▶**US Open (tennis)** – Flushing Meadows - Aug 29- September 11 - usopen.org.

September

▶**Labor Day** – first Mon in Sept.

▶**Brazilian Parade** on Avenue of the Americas (6th Ave.) and **West Indian Day Parade** - first Mon in Sept.

▶**NYC Century Ride** – early September - www.transalt.org - 35, 55, 75, or 110mi bike ride around NYC.

▶**Feast of San Gennaro** – Italian festival in Little Italy - around mid-September.

▶**BAM Next Wave Festival** – Experimental dance, concerts and theatre at Brooklyn Academy of Music - from mid-September to mid-December - www.bam.org.

October

▶**New York Film Festival** – Lincoln Center - until mid October - www.filmlinc.com.

▶**Columbus Day Parade** – Parade on 5th Avenue to celebrate the discovery of America by Christopher Columbus - 2nd weekend of October.

▶**Greenwich Village Halloween Parade** – Legendary celebration of Halloween - October 31.

145

© Y. Saito/Michelin

New York City Marathon

November
▶**New York City Marathon** – first Sun. in Nov.
▶**Veterans Day** or **Armistice Day** – Parade on 5th Avenue - 11 November.
▶**Macy's Thanksgiving Day Parade** – Parade along Broadway, from Central Park West to Herald Square - 4th Thurs in Nov.

December
▶**Tree-Lighting** – Turning on the Christmas lights, particularly in the Rockefeller Center and the corner of 5th Ave./59th St., near Central Park - from December 4.

▶**First Night Festival** – Fireworks in Central Park and South Street Seaport - December 31 - **New Year's Eve Ball Drop** is the big gathering on Times Square, before midnight, where the crowd rings in the New Year as the famous "ball" drops down the *Times building*. It's followed by the **Midnight Run** in Central Park.

BIENNALE

Whitney Biennial – At the Whitney Museum of American Art, you'll find the trends of contemporary art. The biennial is three months every spring, no edition in 2018, the next in 2019 - http://whitney.org/biennial.

BIG EXHIBITIONS

Museums – New York's big museums, such as MoMA (👣 *p. 58*), the Met (👣 *p. 74*), the Whitney (👣 *p. 71*), the Museum of Natural History (👣 *p. 86*) and the Guggenheim (👣 *p. 80*) have major exhibitions all year round. See their websites for calendars.

Things to do in NYC
New York also has many **free papers** and **magazines** *(some below are not free)* with cultural agendas and listings. See *City Guide Magazine* (www.cityguideny.com); *In New York* (www.innewyork.com); *The Skint* (www.theskint.com; *Time Out New York* (www.timeout.com/newyork); *New York* magazine (nymag.com); and the *New Yorker* (www.newyorker.com).

Macy's Thanksgiving Day Parade

Find Out More

Hudson Street, Greenwich Village
© O. Korshakov/Moment/Getty Images

Key dates

1524 - Giovanni da Verrazzano, sent by French king François I, discovers the site of New York.

1609 - Henry Hudson, with the Dutch West India Company explores the river that now takes his name.

1614 - The region becomes a Dutch colony: New Netherland.

1625 - A trading post called New Amsterdam is established at the bottom tip of Manhattan.

1626 - Peter Minuit "buys" Manhattan from the Algonquins.

1636 - Dane Johannes Bronck established a home and farmstead in the area that would become the Bronx.

1644 - Slaves brought by the Dutch in 1626 were freed".

1647 - **Peter Stuyvesant** becomes director-general of the colony.

1653 - He orders the construction of a fortified wall in the location of today's Wall Street.

1657 - Arrival of the English Quakers.

1664 - New Amsterdam is taken by the English and becomes New York.

1667 - Treaty of Breda gives English possession of the colony.

1673 - Holland takes back the city, naming it New Orange.

1674 - Treaty of Westminster returns New Netherland to England.

1725 - William Bradford creates the city's first newspaper, the *New York Gazette*.

1763 - The Treaty of Paris confirms England's domination on the North American continent.

1764-1765 - The Sugar Act and the Stamp Act provoke agitation against the English, leading to the union of nine colonies.

1767 - The "Townsend Taxes" imposed heavily on the colonies cause uproar.

4 July 1767 - Adoption of the **Declaration of Independence**.

1783 - The Treaty of Paris recognizes the independence of the thirteen American colonies. **George Washington** enters triumphantly into New York, which would become the following year the first capital of the United States.

1789 - Washington is elected first president of the United States.

1807 - Fulton links New York to Albany with his steamboat.

1811 - John Randel Jr's plan divides the city into a grid following 12 longitudinal avenues and 155 crossing horizontal roads.

1812 - The United States declares war against Great Britain. New York is affected by the blockade.

1817 - Creation of the Stock Exchange (🔥 p. 156).

1820 - New York is the biggest city in the country (123 706 habitants).

1825 - The Erie Canal links the Great Lakes to the port of New York, which quickly swallows up half the imports for the whole of the United States.

1827 - **Slavery** is abolished in the state of New York.

1835 - A fire ravishes the city.

1845 - The first telegraphic line links New York to Philadelphia.

1851 - Publication of *New York Times*.
1857 - Construction of Central Park begins (📖 *p. 67*).
1861-1865 - American Civil War. Display of the body of **Lincoln** at City Hall after his assassination.
1868 - First overground subway.
1869 - Black Friday and city taken by financial panic.
1872 - Inauguration of the Metropolitan Museum of Art (📖 *p. 74*).
1886 - Inauguration of the **Statue of Liberty** (📖 *p. 22*).
1891 - Inauguration of Carnegie Hall (📖 *p. 52*).
1902 - Completion of Flatiron Building (📖 *p. 49*).
1904 - First underground subway line.
1913 - Duchamp creates a scandal at the first modern art exhibition, the New York Armory Show.
1917-1919 - The US take part in WWI.
1919-1933 - Prohibition of alcohol.
1929 - Wall Street Crash.
1931 - Inauguration of the Empire State Building (📖 *p. 54*).
1939 - Inauguration of Rockefeller Center (📖 *p. 57*).
1941-1945 - Participation of the United States in WWII.
1952 - UN headquarters established in New York.
1965 - Assassination of civil rights activist Malcolm X in Harlem.
1970 - First New York City Marathon.
1973 - Inauguration of the World Trade Center (📖 *p. 14*).
1993 - Explosion of a terrorist bomb at the World Trade Center.
1994 - Rudolph Giuliani becomes mayor.

January 2001 - Hillary Clinton starts her mandate as United States Senator from New York.
11 September 2001 - Terrorist attack and destruction of the World Trade Center: 2,752 dead and missing.
4 July 2004 - First stone of Freedom Tower laid, renamed One World Trade Center.
September 2008 - Fall of Lehman Brothers and financial crisis. Wall Street collapses.
November 2008 - Barack Obama is elected president of the United States.
January 2010 - Michael Bloomberg, elected for the first time in 2002, starts his third mandate as mayor.
2012 - One World Trade Center becomes the highest tower in New York (541m/1,775ft).
29-30 October 2012 - Hurricane Sandy hits New York, leading to 41 deaths and causing $40bn. of damage. The 43rd New York City Marathon is canceled.
November 2012 - Barack Obama re-elected President of the US.
November 2013 - Democrat Bill de Blasio elected as mayor.
November 2016 - Hillary Clinton takes 48% of the popular vote, but Donald Trump is nonetheless elected President of the US.
October 2017 - New York commits to upholding Paris Agreement principles.
November 2017 - New York commits to being a sanctuary city for immigrants and refugees.

151

The Big Apple

A LAND TO CONQUER

Giovanni da Verrazzano, a Florentine explorer serving the French king François I, arrived at the bay of New York in 1524. He baptised the area the "Terre d'Angoulême" (land of Angoulême, a commune in southwestern France) in honor of his feudal overlord from the family of des Valois Angoulême. In 1609, Englishman **Henry Hudson**, a navigator exploring on behalf of the Dutch, would also come to the region. Sailing the river that today carries his name, he encountered Amerindians and left decreeing these territories Dutch property. The traders entered into negotiation with the "Indians" (Native Americans), comprising two groups : the Mohawks from the Iroquois Confederacy, and the Algonquin people, also called "Delaware".

NEW AMSTERDAM

In 1614, Dutch West India Company founded the **colony of New Netherland**, on the site of present-day New York. In 1626, **Peter Minuit** bought Manhattan (from the Algonquin word, *menatay*, meaning "island") from the Wappingers for 60 florins (or just $26!). Racial tensions were created under the pressure of the colonists. The first violence occurred in 1640, against the Algonquins. Subsequently, with each changing alliance, the different Amerindian tribes of the region would participate in the wars between rival settlers.

BIRTH OF A CITY

After constructing fortifications on the southern tip of the island of Manhattan, Dutch engineer **Fredericksz** developed the plans for the future city, New Amsterdam. He would design winding roads with *boweries* (farms) built either side, on often swampy land; the Dutch ancestral experience of drainage worked wonders. Agricultural areas would appear further to the north and in the areas of Brooklyn, Queens, the Bronx and Staten Island. But the great urban construction project was never fully finished. Only the defensive wall would be significant enough that the road that replaced it retained the name, Wall Street. The famous **Peter Stuyvesant** would be the last director-general of this colony. Holland decided to concentrate on Asia, and New Netherland was practically abandoned. In 1664, the town was given to the English without a fight, who would rule over it for 119 years. New Amsterdam was renamed "New York" in honor of the brother of King Charles II, the Duke of York.

Immigration

Attracted by its seemingly limitless development, immigrants started arriving in New York, with new waves coming across as successive wars, political conflicts and economic troubles hit Europe.

THE IRISH WAVE

In 1860, Irish people represented a third of the city's inhabitants. Poor and often illiterate, they were held in disdain by the descendants of the settlers and had to fight to survive. The first known gangs of New York were Irish (see 2002 film *Gangs of New York*). Over time they gained power over the city police. These gangs, which were soon joined by immigrants of other origins—Italian, Jewish, Central American, South American and Asian—would be one of the dominating factors of the life of the city, across every time period.

BLACK HISTORY OF NEW YORK

Less known is the story of the immigration of black people, of which the history is troubled and somewhat murky. In 1626, the Dutch brought enslaved people from Africa, as the English would do later. Several slave markets would prosper on Wall Street. In 1827, the slave trade was officially abolished in New York, but even when legally freed, black people faced many difficulties. Some of the black population formed a new middle class and some, facing discrimination, remained in poverty.

CONTROLLING IMMIGRATION

For most immigrants, New York offered hope of a new life. They were brought over for labour on the huge construction works that were taken place, but were held in suspicion and for society's ills. New Yorkers soon started trying to control the flow of new arrivals. A "sorting office" was first established at Castle Garden, and then **Ellis Island**; 20 000 immigrants passed through here each day, including 16 million Europeans, before it closed in 1924. Many of them were heading to the west of the country, but a good deal settled in New York, causing a sensational rise in population, from 500 000 inhabitants in 1850 to more than 3 million in 1900, making it the most populated city in the world. New York became an emblem of liberty, and Jewish people fleeing persecution were joined by Italian immigrants, and then Chinese people. Rich immigrants had no difficulty getting established in the city, but most of these new arrivals were plunged into a most precarious existence. Communities tended to group together in the same areas (Little Italy, Chinatown, Lower East Side), giving the city its defining diverse identity.

Cosmopolitan New York

A MULTIETHNIC CITY

New York is the most ethnically diverse city in the United States. Walking through the streets you'll hear a cornucopia of languages, especially Spanish, Mandarin and Cantonese. Its wealth of diversity is evident in the huge variety of food served, from burgers to Jamaican curry, Tibetan dumplings to duck confit. The city has more than 8.6 million inhabitants. Almost 37% are foreign born, and nearly 50% speak non-English languages at home. The highest contingent of immigrants today come from the Dominican Republic, China, Jamaica, Guyana and Mexico, though there are also arrivals from Bangladesh, Nigeria, Ghana, the Philippines, Russia and Ukraine.

COMMUNITIES

One of the characteristics of New York is the strong presence of distinct communities. Many visitors are surprised by the specificity of the pockets of the city. Sometimes you just need to cross the road to pass into another continent. The historic communities have often made their areas famous: Jewish people in the Lower East Side, Upper West Side and Williamsburg, Italians in Little Italy (Manhattan) and in the Bronx, and Poles in Greenpoint. Sometimes communities can be found in unexpected places; for example, there are still many people from China in Manhattan's Chinatown, but the area has now been overtaken by Flushing, Queens. Then there are cultural enclaves spread throughout the city, such as Ukrainian "Little Odessa" in Brighton Beach; Koreatown along 32nd Street in Manhattan; the Caribbean areas around Flatbush Avenue in Brooklyn; Dominicans in the Bronx; Senegalese people on 116th Street, between Nicholas and 8th Avenues; a Turkish community, also in Brighton Beach; Brazilians and Greeks in Astoria, Queens, and Indians in Jackson Heights, Queens.

A COSMOPOLITAN CUISINE

There is no single kind of New York cuisine: you'll find everything. If it exists in the world, you'll probably find it in New York. The 20,000-plus restaurants of the city offer classic American fare but also Italian, Jewish, Ukrainian, Korean, Indian, Bangladeshi, Chinese, Cuban, Nigerian, Colombian, South African, Australian and more. The different influences mix too, creating new kinds of cuisine. Some particularly New York foods, like bagels and pizza, will always be staples.

Mexican food stall, Chelsea Market

COS No.1
disfruta
Coca-Cola
BIEN
ORDER HERE!
LOS TACOS
No.1
TAMARINDO
DRINK
Coca-Cola

Economy and Finance

New York owes its rapid development to the exceptional position of its port and the opening of the Erie Canal. Today the port activity is contained to just a few piers.

REAL ESTATE AND INDUSTRY

The building sector has always enjoyed success. In the 1950s and '60s, slums were demolished and large housing complexes were created in their place, while public highways were developed and the bridges and subway lines updated. In the next few decades, the focus would be on preserving the older heritage of the city. Speculation was centered around abandoned industrial sites and ports located beyond the East River. The cost of rent and the competition caused by globalization forced industries out, and jobs fell by half from 1950. Dressmaking and tailoring continued in the Garment District, but the kind of work was now limited to only high-end items. The high education level of the inhabitants of the city and its immigrants favored the development of technology, as well as the medical sector and computing. Food, high-end mechanics and the chemical industries also held up.

PRESS AND ENTERTAINMENT

New York is a bastion of the press, synonymous with independent thinking. The city is the home of no less than 15 newspapers and nearly 300 magazines, as well as press and photo agencies, national television channels and a good number of cable TV channels. The city, where bibliophiles have always been in abundance, is also home to major publishing houses. Countless congresses and conventions are held here. A significant entertainment industry has also developed over the years with the many concert halls, theaters and cabarets. New York is also, of course, the site of some of the most famous museums on the planet.

WALL STREET AND FINANCE

The **New York Stock Exchange** (NYSE), aka Wall Street, is the definitive symbol of capitalism and the world's most important stock market. Brokers trade values of $42bn. every day. A substantial proportion of international finance passes through the hands of these brokers amounting to huge sums, which, in turn act as a waterfall, irrigating the economic networks of New York, in particular the professions attached to finance. These jobs create and maintain in turn a myriad of services at every level of city life.

The world of finance was however severely shaken by the crisis of 2008, which created a new push for the regulation of financial activity.

Design and Architecture

SEARCHING FOR A STYLE

The English turned New York into a North American trading post on the foundations of a Dutch city; along the muddy roads, Georgian-style houses were built with curved eaves, colonnades and pediments.

After their victory over the English, the settlers were inspired by the architecture of the Roman Republic. The **Federal style** was characterized by symmetrical and square constructions, with classical ornamentation, columns sometimes raised on pediments and imposts, as well as the use of elliptical windows. The mayor DeWitt Clinton (1769-1828) was responsible for the planning of the road grid, with avenues laid out at right angles. The Randel Plan, the famous "grid" of Manhattan, with its 2028 blocks, was thus created in 1811. The **neo-Grec style** was all the rage from 1820, characterized by marble and large pediments framed with Doric, Ionic and Corinthian style colonnades (Federal Hall). Churches and whole roads (Cushman Row) were constructed in relativity austere style. But as it was enjoying economic boom, the city was ravaged by a huge fire (1835). The **neo-Gothic style** came next. It plays on asymmetry, the picturesque, the profusion of turrets, niches, and long, narrow oblong-shaped windows. It became the fashion for new mansions, with an emphasis on finely worked gables, spires and gargoyles. A want for excess born of the end of the Victorian era lead to **Queen Anne style**, where yet more ornamentation was added (1880-1905). With a combination of influences mixing Byzantine and medieval, the **neo-Romanesque** style emerged. It was characterized by massive towers and heavy semi-circular arches in cut stone, as well as bas-reliefs, and cast iron gate copies.

INFLUENCES AND ECLECTICISM

As Romantic and Gothic trends developed, architects turned towards Italy and Paris for inspiration. The **Italian style** (1840-1880) also benefited from the use of cast iron in architecture with its rectangular appearance, raised front steps and finely arched narrow windows. In the south part of Manhattan, the use of cast iron allowed for the construction of higher buildings, leading to the creation of the first skyscrapers. Architects and developers would experiment with the assembly of prefabricated iron pieces, slotted with glistening glass once in situ. Houses were often coated in inexpensive chocolate-colored sandstone, giving them their name, "brownstones". By extension the same term would also be applied to the houses of the same areas, built in brick or other kinds of stone.

The French **Second Empire style** (1860-1880) would also influence New York, with zinc rooftops and mansard-style top floors becoming popular. This style was followed by a vogue for **neoclassical and Beaux-Arts**, inspired by Paris, with grand structures featuring arcades and monumental entrances embellished by columns and statues (see main branch of New York Public Library).

CONQUERING THE SKIES

The real revolution would come not so much from changing styles, bur rather the aim to build high into the sky. If the initial motivation was speculative—to fit in the most construction possible in the smallest space available—it was this decision to build ever-higher that changed the look of the city most definitively. In 1857, Elisha Otis invented the elevator. The American Institute of Architects was created in New York in the same year. A little later, a particularly innovative school opened in Chicago, where the first skyscraper would be built. In New York, the **Flatiron Building** (1902) was the first of a series of buildings that would constitute the famous Manhattan skyline. Skyscrapers sprouted up like mushrooms throughout the 20C. A new European fashion, **Art Nouveau**, came over, followed in 1925 by **Art Deco**. The latter was characterized by recesses, playing with vertical harmonies, buildings coated in stone and varnished brick or metal (see Chrysler Building,

Empire State Building). After the Second World War, in reaction to the luxurious tastes of the time, buildings were constructed in **"international" style,** with clean lines, rectilinear layouts and glass walls and surfaces (see UN headquarters, MoMA). The last two decades of the 20C, called **postmodern**, saw the use of features such as iridescent colored glasswork, and stone made a marked comeback in the paving of esplanades and atria (see World Financial Center, World Trade Center, Guggenheim Museum, Whitney Museum).

THE 21ST CENTURY

The collapse of the World Trade Center in 2001, marked a turning point for the city. As well as the symbolic construction of 1 World Trade Center, the whole horizon of New York was also redesigned. The successive closure of the major port spaces left huge virgin terrains, prime for development. The riverbanks of Brooklyn and Queens, with a view over the towers of Midtown, quickly began housing a number of new projects, while in Manhattan towers would shoot up, designed by famous names such as Jean Nouvel, Zaha Hadid and Herzog & de Meuron. Perhaps most significantly, the monumental Hudson Yards began. To accomodate the expansion of the city, a new subway line on 2nd Avenue began opening, and an extension of line 7 was also built.

Flatiron Building

Modern Art

Until the start of the 20C, American painting was inwards-looking, turning towards nature or society.

THE EIGHT

It was in February 1908 that a thunderbolt would amplify the impressionist revolution in America. Seven young painters, brought together around **Robert Henry**, would exhibit at the Macbeth Gallery. They painted the smoke and the grime of the city, the exhaustion of the workers, and lust, and proved that there was beauty to be found in sweat and tears. This earned them the nickname **Ashcan School** (from ash can). This movement was followed by a period of artistic tumult, which would reach its zenith at the Exhibition of Independent Artists (1910) and especially at the Armory Show (1913), the largest art exhibition ever held in the United States.

THE AMERICAN AVANT-GARDE

Marcel Duchamp presented his *Nude Descending a Staircase* in the US which would create a public scandal, but would help his fellow painters in their experiments. In a few short but crucial years, the gallery of Alfred Stieglitz on 5th Avenue would exhibit **Georgia O'Keeffe** and **Arthur Dove**, the first American abstract artist, as well as **Charles Demuth** and **Charles Sheeler**, specialists in urban hyperrealism

THE GREAT FIGURES

New York was suddenly cast into the spotlight by the work of **Edward Hopper**, whose art was a remarkable meditation on modern American life. During the Great Depression, **Thomas Benton**, **Grant Wood**, **Reginald Marsh**, **Ben Shahn** and **John Curry** would examine the American way of life. In 1936, Mark Rothko, Arshile Gorky, Willem De Kooning, Robert Motherwell and Jackson Pollock would form the core of the **American Abstract Artists** (AAA). They constituted, after 1945, the first school of painting with international reach; abstract expressionism was also known as the "New York School". With the addition of famous artists forced to flee across the Atlantic during the War, such as **Léger**, **Miró** and **Ernst**, they would turn the artistic landscape on its head. In 1958, **Leo Castelli** opened in the Upper East Side his reputation-making gallery (Castelli Gallery). A new generation of artists was born. **Andy Warhol** and pop art would change the face of contemporary art, which would move into the streets. New York now had a strong place in the art market; public spaces would welcome work by Dubuffet, Tony Rosenthal, Henry Moore, Jim Dine, Fritz Koenig and Milton Hebald.

The Legend of Broadway

In the **Theater District**, there are around 40 venues with 500 seats, of which more than two thirds show only musicals; this ensemble constitutes the official Broadway, or "on Broadway". Hugely successful and popular shows run in these theaters. Below 500 seats, venues are called "off Broadway" and welcome young and starting actors. For actors, performing on Broadway is synonymous with recognition.

THE THEATER

Eugene O'Neill (1888-1953), born in New York, is the most famous North American playwright. Throughout his career, he would explore the darkest aspects of the human condition, with his plays exploring a world of marginalized people and despair. **John Steinbeck** (*Of Mice and Men*, 1937), is highly acclaimed by many for his works. **Arthur Miller** (1915-2005) wrote short-form plays, such as *Death of a Salesman* (1949) and *The Crucible* (1953). Among more contemporary writers, **Sam Shepard**, writer, screenwriter and actor, is also a well-regarded playwright, from the writing of his sketches for theatrical revue *O! Calcutta*. **August Wilson** (1945-2005), two-time winner of the Pulitzer Prize for *Fences* and *The Piano Lesson*, was a great Afro-American writer, describing through a series of ten plays (*The Pittsburgh Cycle*), aspects of the African-American experience over a period of 100 years. **Wendy Wasserstein** (1950-2006), born in Brooklyn, was another major playwright and winner of the Pulitzer Prize for Drama in 1989 for *The Heidi Chronicles.*

MUSICAL THEATER

The section of Broadway in line with Times Square has become a place of legend. The first musical, *The Black Crook*, played to sold-out crowds in 1866. Encouraged by its success, producers would develop this genre. In the 1920s and '30s, one musical followed another and their songs became huge hits. **Fred Astaire** and **Gene Kelly** danced on to people's cinema screens. Musicals reached a zenith in 1957, Stephen Sondheim's *West Side Story*, with music composed by Leonard Bernstein, made its premiere at the Winter Garden. The legend of Romeo and Juliet was transposed onto the working-class areas of 1950s New York, creating a sensational success. For some years now, many musicals have been inspired by the films of Walt Disney, such as *The Lion King* and *Mary Poppins,* but also more varied themes, such as the legendary *Les Misérables,* adapted from a novel by Victor Hugo. *Cats* has been performed more than 9 000 times since its creation in 1981. Today, *The Book of Mormon* and *Hamilton* are among some of the shows taking center stage.

Andy Warhol and Pop Art

POP ART

Roy Lichtenstein, **Robert Rauschenberg**, **Jasper Johns** and especially Andy Warhol and the ultra-cool coterie that frequented his Factory were the principal players of pop art, the motor of a frenetic speculative machine that made New York the world capital of the art market. Drawing inspiration from the ad houses for which they worked, from comic strips and the current affairs of their time, Andy Warhol and Roy Lichtenstein made everyday life the subject of their art. Their totally innovative and easy-to-reproduce art centered around real-life objects and they approached their subjects mechanically, using repetition and mixing colors to create a subtle harmony.

ANDY WARHOL (1928-1987)

He started out drawing advertisements for magazines and looking after the displays of a department store. He very quickly carried out his first canvasses, taking inspiration from comic strips. His bottles of Coca-Cola and Campbell's soup cans were a dramatic success. He moved into silkscreen printing, which would allow him to reproduce his subjects as many times as he liked. He won recognition immediately. A loft, the Factory, was his workshop.

A multitude of collaborators helped him to create his ideas from his sketches. Cold, cynical and intelligent, he was held in adulation by the New York jet-set, as well as regular New-Yorkers who identified with the themes his work explored. He undertook a series of now-iconic, portraits: Marilyn Monroe, Elvis Presley, Jackie Kennedy, Mao Zedong and Lenin, as well as Mona Lisa and huge multicolored repeated flower prints. Passionate about the tools of cinematography, he directed a number of art films featuring improvising characters.

AFTER POP ART

The wild spike in prices and the unequal nature and quality of exhibitions formed a bubble that would suck in investors. Art became snobbish and it would be felt in the quality of the work. From this profusion of work, occasionally a pearl would emerge, such as **Jean-Michel Basquiat** (1960-1988) whose raging and hallucinatory genius, synthesized different cultural references and pop art, with the style he developed as a street artist and tagger in New York. At this time, many working-class areas (Harlem, Bronx, Queens) were covered in murals, becoming ephemeral open-air galleries.

Mural by Nychos the Weird in Bushwick, Brooklyn

Literature

Writers who were born or lived in New York, such as Herman Melville, were not always inspired by their own city. From the 19C onwards, however **Washington Irving** wrote *A History of New York* (1809), **Stephen Crane** caused a scandal with New York street slang in *Maggie: A Girl of the Streets* (1893); **Edith Wharton** (1862-1937) offered superb descriptions of New York high society in *The House of Mirth* (1905) and *The Age of Innocence* (1920). **F. Scott Fitzgerald** described the New York of the Roaring Twenties and the corruption of the American dream in *The Great Gatsby* (1925).

MANHATTAN: CITY OF THE THRILLER

With *Manhattan Transfer* (1925) by **John Dos Passos**, the New York literature of the 20C was born, as was the case in Europe with *Ulysses* by James Joyce and *Journey to the End of the Night* by Céline. *Manhattan Transfer* is a comprehensive work, run through with jazz rhythms and the explosion of Cubist painting. New York appears like a well-oiled machine where chaos reigns. A kind of literature tried to make sense of this disorder: the noir novel and the thriller. *City of the Dead* by Herbert Lieberman (1991), *The Alienist* by Caleb Carr (1995) and *Bone* by George Chesbro (1993) would give back some faith in humanity. **Dashiell Hammett**, creator of the great Sam Spade, one of literature's most iconic private detectives (*The Maltese Falcon*, 1929), described like no other the corruption of the city in a distinctive pared-down style. **Chester Himes** with *The Five Cornered Square* (1958) would inaugurate the Harlem patrols of black cops Coffin Ed Johnson and Gravedigger Jones.

BEYOND GENRES

Writers and poets would naturally begin to meet to exchange ideas. **Greenwich Village** welcomed Mark Twain, Henry James, Melville and the playwright Eugene O'Neill, the poet Edna St Vincent Millay, Theodore Dreiser and Thomas Wolfe. Dylan Thomas was followed by the **Beat Generation**, defined by names such as William Burroughs, Allen Ginsberg and Jack Kerouac. The most famous of these circles would be the **Algonquin Round Table**, named after a hotel bar, where the members of prestigious *The New Yorker* would make and unmake reputations. Public readings were held amid the cultural circle and literary prizes, like the **Pulitzer** and the **National Book Award**, were awarded. Some writers would keep their distance from the media such as J.D. Salinger (1951-2010), author of *The Catcher in the Rye*.

Among famous literary New-Yorkers are Tom Wolfe, Truman Capote, Joan Didion, Nora Ephron, Grace Paley, Toni Morrison, Hubert Selby Jr., Jay McInerney and Paul Auster.

Filming New York

In the beginnings of the film industry, the Eastman-Edison trust would shoot its films in greater New York. But in 1908, its competitors left for Hollywood, where prices were lower and space more readily available. New York remained a photogenic site, appreciated by directors and would still be the backdrop of various films and televised series.

CINEMA INDUSTRY

Despite the attraction of Hollywood, independent filmmakers chose to work in New York: John Cassavetes, Abel Ferrara, Amos Kollek, Jim Jarmusch, Spike Lee, Martin Scorsese and Woody Allen, who made an icon of Manhattan in his films.

The creation in 1947 of the Actors Studio in New York marked a turning point in the history of New York cinema. It would train a whole host of stars, including Marlon Brando, James Dean and Robert De Niro, a favorite of Martin Scorsese. The city houses some of the best film schools—the Tisch School of the Arts at NYU, the School of Visual Arts, the New School and the film departments of Columbia University— as well as the **American Museum of the Moving Image** (ⓒ *p. 100*). Distribution has also progressed a great deal. Well-equipped cinema spaces have blossomed and festivals attract enthusiasts : Dance on Camera Festival (Feb), **Tribeca Film Festival**, run by De Niro (May), Human Rights Watch Film Festival (June), New York Film Festival (Sep-Oct) NewFest : New York LGBT Film Festival (Oct), Williamsburg Independent Film Festival (Nov).

FROM CINEMA TO TELEVISION

The renaissance of New York's film studios owes a lot to television, and it's now very uncommon to see filming around the city. Cult series such as *Sex and the City, The Sopranos, Gossip Girl* and *NYPD* were known to huge audiences and many still make pilgrimages to filming locations featured in them. As well as series, the entertainment show *Saturday Night Live,* broadcast live every Saturday night, is another televisual event. It launched stars including Bill Murray, Kristen Wiig and Tina Fay.

LEGENDARY SITES

The cinema of New York has created some powerful images over the years, such as King Kong climbing the **Empire State Building**. Hitchcock showed Cary Grant attempting to escape his pursuers at the **Plaza Hotel** (*North by Northwest*, 1959); you may also remember Dustin Hoffman running around **Central Park** reservoir (*Marathon Man*, 1976). A more romantic atmosphere floats around Woody Allen and Diane Keaton in front of the fountain in Bryant Park in *Manhattan* (1979).

Music

CLASSICAL MUSIC

As well as the Metropolitan Opera House, the city offers Carnegie Hall and Lincoln Center. The biggest soloists and opera singers regularly perform the works of renowned composers such as Dvořák and Tchaikovsky.

THE SYMBOL OF AMERICA

Though jazz originated in New Orleans at the end of the 19C, New York welcomed its greatest creators. Jazz and dance clubs blossomed in the 1920s in Harlem. The Cotton Club, on Lenox Avenue, received **Duke Ellington**, **Count Basie** and **Cab Calloway**. In 1924, **George Gershwin** performed his jazz-style piece *Rhapsody in Blue*. Later, a number of significant clubs could be found on 52nd Street, without it dethroning Harlem; this was where **Ella Fitzgerald** triumphed in 1935. **Gospel** shook the churches of New York with its rousing rhythms. Lester Young and Coleman Hawkins enjoyed the heyday of the **swing** period in New York. From 1945-1948, the **bebop revolution** , animated by **Dizzy Gillespie** and **Charlie Parker** unfolded throughout the city. Modern jazz would be built on its foundations, characterized by geniuses such as **Thelonious Monk**, **John Coltrane** and **Miles Davis**. New York is also

where the devotees of **free jazz** were recruited in the 1960s and 70s, before the advent of the contemporary period of jazz. Today, all the genre's iterations can be found in New York, from the most conventional at Lincoln Center to trendy clubs and open-air summer festivals

ROCK, FOLK, PUNK, RAP

If the **Velvet Underground** were the standard bearers, some New York rock groups also could or can rival their British counterparts; talents span a range of styles (Ramones, New York Dolls, Sonic Youth, The Strokes, Pavement, Interpol and more recently MGMT and Vampire Weekend). **Patti Smith** and **Lou Reed** brought a poetic touch to the starker sound of the scene, and quality recording studios often attract top artists. The city itself also inspires artists such as Norah Jones, Bob Dylan, U2 and Simon & Garfunkel, who celebrate it in their songs. *New York, New York* (sung by Frank Sinatra) is perhaps the most famous song about the city. New York is also the city of rappers and **hip-hop** (Jay-Z, Nas, Mase, Public Enemy) who tell the story of New York street life, chiming culturally with street art. Today you'll often see rap performances in the streets of Manhattan.

Saxophonist in front of Carnegie Hall

Maps

Inside

Cover
Neighborhoods of New York
Inside front cover

Photo credits

Page 4
Greenwich Village: © lavendertime/iStockphoto.com
Central Park: © J. Arnold Images/hemis.fr
Museum of Modern Art © T. Hamburg/imageBROKER/age fotostock
One World Observatory: © Alex Spatari/Moment Open/Getty Images
Metropolitan Museum of Art: © L. Decoudin/Michelin

Page 5
Empire State Building: © L. Decoudin/Michelin
Brooklyn Bridge: © kasto80/iStockphoto.com
Times Square: © J. D. Price/Moment/Getty Images
Soho: © Ch. Heeb/hemis.fr
Statue of Liberty: © Jon Arnold/hemis.fr

short-stay

- ♦ Charleston
- ♦ London
- ♦ New Orleans
- ♦ New York
- ♦ Paris

Visit your preferred bookseller for the short-stay series, plus Michelin's comprehensive range of Green Guides, maps, and famous red-cover Hotel and Restaurant guides.

THEGREENGUIDE short-stays **New York**

Editorial Director	Cynthia Ochterbeck
Editor	Sophie Friedman
Translator	Alexandra Shelton
Production Manager	Natasha George
Cartography	Peter Wrenn, Nicolas Breton
Picture Editor	Yoshimi Kanazawa
Interior Design	Laurent Muller
Layout	Natasha George

Contact Us

Michelin Travel and Lifestyle North America
One Parkway South
Greenville, SC 29615
USA
travel.lifestyle@us.michelin.com

Michelin Travel Partner
Hannay House
39 Clarendon Road
Watford, Herts WD17 1JA
UK
☏01923 205240
travelpubsales@uk.michelin.com
www.viamichelin.co.uk

Special Sales

For information regarding bulk sales,
customized editions and premium sales,
please contact us at:
travel.lifestyle@us.michelin.com

Tell us
what you think
about our products.

Give us your opinion:

satisfaction.michelin.com

Michelin Travel Partner

Société par actions simplifiées au capital de 11 288 880 EUR
27 cours de l'Ile Seguin - 92100 Boulogne Billancourt (France)
R.C.S. Nanterre 433 677 721

No part of this publication may be reproduced in any form
without the prior permission of the publisher.

© Michelin Travel Partner
ISBN 978-2-067230-24-8
Printed: April 2018
Printer: GEERS